There is now a broad consensus on the need for greater reliance on private enterprise and markets to promote growth in developing countries. The OECD Development Assistance Committee (DAC) has intensified its work on the role of the aid system in encouraging productive private sectors and foreign direct investment.

This study describes DAC Members' policies and programmes for private sector development. Part I contains recommendations agreed by the DAC on means of improving international co–operation for private sector development and foreign direct investment in developing countries. Part II surveys Members' efforts to promote productive enterprise and investment in recipient countries. It draws upon work by the DAC, the World Bank Group and others, as well as the results of missions to developing countries undertaken by the DAC in 1988–89. Part III is a country–by–country description of what DAC Members and international agencies are doing to promote foreign direct investment in developing countries; it absorbs and expands the previous OECD publication *Investing in Developing Countries*, fifth revised edition, Paris 1983.

The study is published under the responsibility of the Secretary–General.

Also available

INTERNATIONAL DIRECT INVESTMENT AND THE NEW ECONOMIC ENVIRONMENT. The Tokyo Round Table (1989)
(21 89 03 1) ISBN 92-64-13289-9, 148 pp.   £12.00   US$21.00   FF100   DM41

DEVELOPMENT CO–OPERATION IN THE 1990s. 1989 REVIEW. Efforts and Policies of the Member of the Development Assistance Committee. Report by Joseph C. Wheeler, Chairman of the Development Assistance Committee (1989)
(43 89 04 1) ISBN 92-64-13300-3, 258 pp.   £18.00   US$32.00   FF150   DM62

FINANCING AND EXTERNAL DEBT OF DEVELOPING COUNTRIES – 1988 SURVEY (1989)
(43 89 03 1) ISBN 92-64-13261-9, 228 pp.   £14.50   US$25.00   FF120   DM50

Development Centre Studies

THE WORLD ECONOMY IN THE 20th CENTURY by Angus Maddison (1989)
(41 89 05 1) ISBN 92-64-13274-0, 160 pp.   £17.00   US$30.00   FF140   DM58

NEW FORMS OF INVESTMENT IN DEVELOPING COUNTRY INDUSTRIES: Mining, Petrochemicals, Automobiles, Textiles, Food (1989)
(41 89 02 1) ISBN 92-64-13188-4, 276 pp.   £28.00   US$48.50   FF230   DM95

FINANCIAL POLICIES AND DEVELOPMENT by Jacques J. Polak (1989)
(41 89 01 1) ISBN 92-64-13187-6, 234 pp.   £17.00   US$29.50   FF140   DM58

RECYCLING JAPAN'S SURPLUSES FOR DEVELOPING COUNTRIES by T. Ozawa (1989)
(41 88 05 1) ISBN 92-64-13177-9, 114 pp.   £11.00   US$19.00   FF90   DM37

TABLE OF CONTENTS

I

ENHANCED INTERNATIONAL CO–OPERATION IN PRIVATE SECTOR DEVELOPMENT AND FOREIGN INVESTMENT IN DEVELOPING COUNTRIES: RECOMMENDED POLICIES AND ACTIONS

During the 1980s, the development of the private sector moved from the margins to the center of economic development strategies in many developing countries. A new pragmatism largely replaced earlier doctrinal objections to an expanding role for the private sector. In most countries, the change of political climate permitted more active encouragement of foreign direct investment. Rationalisation or privatisation of selected state enterprises (parastatals) became an important feature of many national strategies. Economic necessity and lessons of experience with state enterprises drove the new realism. The guidance of the main international financial institutions in the drafting of economic adjustment programmes and their support of policies to accelerate the growth and diversification of economically rational production and exports have been the main external influences towards greater reliance upon market forces and private enterprise.

The commitment of developing countries to increase their reliance upon market disciplines and private enterprise is creating improved opportunities for constructive international co–operation. Responding to these opportunities, Members of the Development Assistance Committee (DAC) and several multilateral development agencies have been considering how to give more comprehensive and effective support for private sector development, including the promotion of foreign direct investment.

Drawing upon the experience of Members of the DAC, major multilateral agencies and selected developing countries, this study suggests conceptual and procedural approaches to accelerating the development of the private sector. It defines the scope of activities that may be required and describes means by which a developing country could determine its own priorities for action and for external assistance. Recognizing the wide diversity of developing countries, no single set of measures is proposed. Rather, the study recommends a set of measures that are likely to increase the contributions of conventional development assistance activities to the growth of a country's private sector. It also proposes measures to maximise the effectiveness of aid activities specially designed to promote foreign direct investment.

While recognising diverse country circumstances, the DAC has concluded that several general principles are applicable to all countries seeking to enhance private sector contributions to growth, production, employment and revenues. The most important prerequisite is a strong, competent government, capable of delivering essential public services and maintaining coherent, growth–oriented economic policies and an effective and transparent regulatory and legal framework. A second common principle is that a development project which cannot be sustained except with public subsidy (including trade protection or monopoly privileges) must be appraised with special caution because of the risks of market and development distortions. Support of an enterprise which is not commercially viable will deter foreign private investment. Finally, since sustainable economic growth depends heavily on successful exploitation of comparative advantage through trade, the economic environment for trade–based enterprise development must be of concern to all development partners.

The recommendations set out below reflect the current state of DAC discussions. They are subject to evolution as practical experience and lessons provide new insights and DAC work proceeds. The DAC will work with relevant OECD committees, in particular the Committee on International Investment and Multinational Enterprises (CIME), in promoting foreign direct investment and private sectors in developing countries.

1. CO–OPERATION FOR PRIVATE SECTOR DEVELOPMENT

The following components of private sector development have been identified and will be developed more fully below:

- i) Encouragement and support of economic policy adjustments designed to induce private investment, stimulate productive enterprise, and facilitate economically sound exports;
- ii) Technical assistance in the design and execution of phased deregulation or reduction of governmental interventions in business, and of legal reforms which strengthen the government's capacity to promote competitive markets, prevent abuses by monopolies, protect the environment, and ensure that the results of growth are equitably shared;
- iii) Measures to expand the availability of investment funds to private enterprises, including long–term efforts to develop efficient banking and other financial market institutions in developing countries;
- iv) Improvement of export promotion services (export–orientation is often an important determinant of the quality of a domestic or foreign investment project and its contribution to economic growth);
- v) Technical assistance, financing, and guarantee programmes to help developing countries improve their investment promotion services or to attract particular foreign investments;
- vi) Financial and technical co–operation in the development of infrastructure and training required by private enterprise or by an export campaign substantially dependent upon private enterprise;
- vii) Strengthening of institutions or programmes serving structurally weak entrepreneurs in a developing country, such as small or micro–enterprises and businesswomen, particularly by facilitating their access to credit;
- viii) Advice and financial aid to the rationalisation or privatisation of selected state–owned enterprises (parastatals);
- ix) Co–operation in enlarging the role of the private sector in providing basic social services and infrastructure.

This list reflects the lessons of many countries' experience in structural adjustment and sectoral development programmes. Policy reforms to establish a coherent economic environment conducive to private enterprise development are essential, but they are not sufficient. "Getting prices right" is only the first requirement of private sector development. The other listed measures, which entail institutional improvements, are also required in many countries. Country–based co–ordination among the national economic agencies and between them and the external assistance agencies is essential to private sector development.

Those activities that require interactions between public agencies and private entrepreneurs are helpful primarily to "formal sector" companies. The liberalisation of economic policies and regulatory regimes, however, and at least some aspects of infrastructure development, are also essential to enabling "informal sector" micro–enterprises to grow, move into the formal economy, and consequently take advantage of official assistance activities.

While most of these activities are primarily designed to serve indigenous private enterprise, they will also encourage foreign direct investment. This dual benefit stems from the fact that a major consideration in investment decisions is usually whether the country's own private businesses are currently investing at home and growing and whether the country offers an expanding "commercial infrastructure".

2. ORIENTATIONS FOR IMPROVING PRIVATE SECTOR DEVELOPMENT

a) Country Strategies

A developing country's priorities for private sector development may be determined through a national strategy or within a development plan. A national strategy may evolve as an aspect of a structural adjustment programme or a set of sectoral development programmes or an export campaign. In any of these cases the nation's goals will usually require a major expansion and diversification of private production, exports and/or economically rational import substitution. In the absence of such an impetus, a government may be induced by the logic of its own economic projections or the example of more successful economies to look to private enterprise to make greater contributions to growth and social services.

Whatever the immediate stimulus to seek stronger private sector development, the most efficient way to determine what needs to be done is to make a comprehensive assessment of the country's main impediments to private investment and enterprise growth in its policies, institutions, infrastructure and other aspects of its environment. Such assessments should take into account concerns expressed by local and foreign businessmen (including those denied opportunity), by labour leaders and other informed persons. Efforts to help these and micro entrepreneurs, including female entrepreneurs, identify their own needs will contribute to a more informed assessment. External assistance in making assessments, preferably before programmes are launched but also during their evolution, can help to make more effective any subsequent assistance in particular aspects of private sector development. Assessments should be made under the auspices of a country's central economic authorities and engage interested ministries and local businessmen, researchers and foreign experts, and investors.

The World Bank/UNDP sponsored consultative groups and round tables are among the appropriate fora to encourage, advise and otherwise assist developing countries to make the assessments described above, and to discuss and follow up on specific issues regarding private enterprise development.

In assisting developing countries to plan and carry out strategies or individual programmes or projects for private enterprise development, DAC Members and multilateral agencies should take fully into account the distinctive economic, cultural and political factors of each country.

b) Economic Policy Reform

Country programmes of economic adjustment should be based on an economic policy environment (especially with respect to exchange rates and foreign exchange management, interest rates and tax policy) that will encourage private savings, and economically rational industrial and agricultural investment and export, and will discourage capital flight.

External aid to a country undertaking a significant liberalisation of foreign exchange and import regimes should be adapted to help in strengthening public and market confidence. This often entails providing foreign exchange through the central bank for current import financing. For a country whose capacity to bear external debt is very limited and which has adopted a sound adjustment programme, supplementary import assistance may be a productive use of aid. Such assistance should be quickly disbursable and accessible to private enterprises.

c) Deregulation/Liberalisation

Structural adjustment programmes and private enterprise development programmes should address the key regulatory (including legal) constraints to their goals, such as barriers to entry or exit from a field of production, labour laws imposing excessive costs on job creation, complex procedures for licensing businesses, and rules which effectively restrict competition and initiative, especially where regulations are used by public officials to harrass or extract corrupt payments from business. The assessment also should identify and weigh the consequences of any absence of clear policies and regulations for private enterprise, including failure to provide for competition, or for protecting the environment or the rights of workers. Action plans to reduce or remove such regulatory impediments to private sector development, to cure regulatory omissions, to reconcile objectives, and to provide for the timing of reform measures should be determined by the country's political leadership and then be incorporated in structural adjustment or other development co-operation agreements.

Before announcing any liberalisation measure, support by political leaders, public officials, business spokesmen, the press and other opinion-makers should be carefully cultivated. Recognising that deregulation deprives some favoured businesses of advantages, those who stand to benefit from liberalisation should be enlisted as advocates of the planned measures.

In order to demonstrate the case for deregulation, the comparative benefits and costs should be assessed and publicised. Often the costs of maintaining regulations are not well understood, even among officials, while the temporary negative effects of liberalisation on previously protected sectors are common knowledge.

The pace of deregulation should take into account the need in some countries to demonstrate the benefits of liberalisation and expand the ranks of supporters before undertaking action requiring legislation.

d) Financing Private Enterprise Development

Financial market development requires a wide range of policy and institutional measures, sometimes requiring phasing and trade–offs. Aid agencies should encourage and assist developing–country authorities to design and secure the adoption of multi-year national strategies for financial market development, including specific measures and action plans.

Financial market development should strengthen incentives for private savings and deter capital flight and should foster market–based allocation of credit through primary reliance upon realistic interest rates rather than administrative controls.

In providing non–project aid to a structural adjustment or sectoral development programme, donors should offer to expand the supply of long–term investment funds for private enterprise as well as to support the current import needs of the country or one of its economic sectors. Counterpart funds derived from non–project aid or two-step loans or grants through the central bank to a qualified intermediate credit institution normally can serve both purposes and simultaneously strengthen the local financial institution. (A two–step loan or grant provides concessional terms for the recipient government or the local bank that is to administer lending of the funds to eligible borrowers but requires or permits application of local market interest rates to the local bank's loan of the funds.) External agencies should provide technical assistance to the local financial institution managing such funds to enable it to make effective use of the additional capital, especially in project appraisals, pricing of sub–loans, and collection of interest and principal.

If DAC Members consider the direct use of aid funds in financing the development of a foreign enterprise, so as to induce foreign direct investment in fields or forms of business activity that have a demonstrated developmental value and entail high commercial risk which a commercial investor would be reluctant to incur, the provisions of paragraph 25, "Appropriate Terms", of the agreed DAC Principles for Project Appraisal ("DAC Principles for Project Appraisal" OECD Paris, 1988) should be applied. This provision reads as follows: "The principal rationale for concessional terms of financial assistance is the recipient country's economic situation and especially limitations on its capacity to mobilise adequate foreign exchange resources for development, rather than the nature of the project financed. In setting terms for end–users, care is required to avoid distorting effects on resource use allocations and income distribution. Two–step financing procedures are a useful device to avoid such distortions; i.e., the project would be expected to carry domestic market interest rates while the concessionary element would accrue to the central government. This is important in the case of revenue–producing projects and particularly projects producing for competitive markets. Project appraisal would make it possible to decide whether it may be justified to pass on all or part of the concessionality in terms to end–users on social or infant industry grounds. But such practices should be consistent with the recipient's broader or sectoral policies; and financial sustainability and equity considerations must also be kept in mind." These principles need to be applied flexibly with due regard to the diversity of local situations.

Technical assistance to financial market development should be supported by research which clarifies all of the major features of the country's financial markets, including the informal financial sector's sources of funds and credit extensions.

DAC Members' public development finance corporations and the International Finance Corporation, the World Bank's private sector arm, should help to develop the competence of private investment finance institutions in developing countries by cofinancing projects and providing in–service training to them.

Further DAC work will address the problems of providing adequate financial resources for private sector development. Problems to be taken up include strengthening financial institutions in developing countries (both development banks and commercial banks) for the mobilisation of savings (and the repatriation of flight capital) and their effective use, and the problems of financial intermediation of official development assistance into the private sector, including, more specifically, small and medium–sized enterprises.

e) Export Promotion

Developing countries should be encouraged to ensure close co–operation between their institutions responsible for export promotion and investment promotion. Inasmuch as these functions require the same type of expertise and personality — the kinds of staff that governments find difficult to recruit and retain at official salary scales — a high degree of interchange or dual assignment of staff may be practicable. Delegation of some or all of these functions to a privately managed and staffed organisation, subject to the government's policy direction, should be considered. The export promotion service should be so conducted as to earn fees from aided companies and associations and to merit subsidies or staff supplementation grants by the government or development assistance agencies.

Technical assistance to export promotion organisations, such as in market and cost analyses and matching exporters and importers, should assist specific segments of production and marketing chains, with priority to subsectors in which local companies have received export orders, rather than augment programmes of generalised and diffused promotion. Export promotion programmes of developing country governments should be encouraged to concentrate on a) making broad assessments of comparative advantage in particular subsectors but not detailed calculations of comparative global production costs of industrial products, leaving such detailed analyses to industrial specialists employed by industry associations, trading companies or foreign investors; b) furnishing to local industrial associations or chambers of commerce current foreign market reports until they are able to assume the costs of gathering market information; c) financing or providing training on practical aspects of international trade in local business schools and in–service training programmes.

Technical assistance on overseas marketing to individual exporters is best provided by trading companies or "downstream" producers with well developed foreign market channels, under either contractual or joint venture arrangements with the producer in a developing country. External agencies of development co–operation may in some countries need to promote such private business arrangements.

Donors should help trade and industrial authorities and economic research bodies of developing countries, including chambers of commerce and industry, to build their own capacities to analyse the export opportunities or competition that may be created by the current round of multilateral trade negotiations and by prospective technological developments.

f) Foreign Investment Promotion

DAC Members and multilateral development assistance agencies have pursued a range of promotional measures and incentives for encouraging foreign direct investment. They are set out comprehensively in Part III. These bilateral and multilateral programmes to promote investment in developing countries should be actively pursued. This section puts forward a number of specific new proposals.

Donors should encourage governments of developing countries to separate their management and staffing of investment promotion from investment regulation. Promotion and regulation require different kinds of personnel and respond to different rewards; regulation tends to crowd out promotion in the allocation of efforts.

DAC Members should exchange views with the Foreign Investment Advisory Service (FIAS) of the International Finance Corporation (IFC) and Multilateral Investment Guarantee Agency (MIGA), and with the UN Industrial Development Organisation (UNIDO), in considering requests for technical assistance to investment-promotion agencies. FIAS provides expert advice to developing countries on legal and regulatory regimes for investment, and other foreign investment policy issues and investment promotion systems. Members also should encourage the use of MIGA's consultative forum for exchange of experience among managers of investment promotion and regulation.

DAC Members and international agencies should demonstrate the positive effects upon foreign investors of protecting intellectual property rights and consistent and predictable investment legislation and enforcement.

g) Infrastructure and Training for Private Sector Development

Basic infrastructure development is often a precondition for increased domestic and foreign investment. In reviewing a developing country's annual infrastructure investment programme during an aid co-ordination exercise, the essential needs of private enterprise development and export development for infrastructure and training should be assessed and provision made for them in the programme.

Infrastructure required to enhance a developing country's attractiveness to foreign investors should be discussed by external agencies (including export credit agencies) with the central economic development authorities of the country in the framework of the national infrastructure investment programme, rather than externally financed in a manner that evades and undermines the public investment budget's discipline.

In order to concentrate public investment resources on infrastructure that only governments can reasonably provide, assistance agencies should encourage consideration of "build-operate-transfer" infrastructure projects through co-operation between foreign private investors and national public or private companies. For the same reason, conventional foreign private investment in such services as air cargo handling should also be encouraged. Privately and publicly financed infrastructure projects should be carefully assessed as to their effects on income distribution.

Assistance agencies should foster the development of indigenous professional services to enterprises — especially legal, accounting, marketing, industrial, economic

13

analysis and environmental assessment and protection services — through training programmes, consultants on aid–financed projects and studies, grants to help establish or strengthen professional associations, and other means. Programmes to upgrade local skills should include professional women.

Country–specific aid co–ordination bodies should review manpower planning systems and manpower development programmes in the developing countries concerned, with a view to avoiding manpower constraints on exports or on crucial private enterprise operations or private investments. Such reviews, which normally should be initiated by the UNDP upon the request of the developing country, may identify requirements for aid either in projecting manpower supply and demand or in supporting the immediate training needs of enterprises and the longer–term development of local institutions for education and training of enterprise staffs.

External agencies and governments of developing countries should encourage local private enterprise and foreign investors to accept larger roles in the provision of advanced training for business and financial managers and other professionals required by enterprises as well as in vocational training closely linked to their enterprise operations.

h) Small Business Development

Independent assessments of the effectiveness of programmes of technical assistance to small entrepreneurs should normally precede the commitment of external aid to these programmes. A practical alternative to delaying a new programme pending such an assessment may be to design the programme as a set of pilot projects. Some of these projects might focus on strengthening the entrepreneurial capacities of disadvantaged groups, many of whom are women.

External agencies should encourage foreign investment enterprises to raise the capacity of small–scale local suppliers of production inputs and finished goods to meet market requirements by providing them with technical assistance, designs, credit or equipment under contracts or joint venture arrangements. To this end, contractual forms of foreign investment or guaranteed offtake contracts should be promoted. DAC Members and multilateral agencies should not, however, endorse or encourage the imposition by host governments on entrepeneurs of requirements to keep arbitrary proportions of production inputs on the local market.

National associations of larger industrialists should be encouraged to promote contractual ties between large and small local producers or distributors ("foster parent" linkages) as a means of stimulating the growth and technological modernisation of small enterprises.

Donors should encourage and assist with technical aid and initial budgetary support the establishment of national associations of small enterprises and women entrepreneurs. Assistance may include special project support, such as co–operative training programmes, research on the impact of public policies and regulations on their businesses, and employment of local counsel to advocate professionally the association's interests to governmental authorities and legislatures.

i) Rationalisation and Privatisation of State Enterprises

Development assistance should be offered to strengthen a developing country's capacity to manage a state enterprise rationalisation and divestment programme.

Expatriate experts and the training of national staffs may be needed in economic and financial analysis of enterprises selected for reform, liquidation or privatisation, selection of the form of privatisation (e.g., public or private sale of shares, sale of assets, dilution of government ownership through new private investment), valuation of shares or assets to be offered for sale, assessment of private bidders and the conditions attached to their bids, analysis of the results of the selected reforms, etc. External aid agencies, especially multilateral ones, can be politically helpful by taking public responsibility for the evaluation of a state enterprise offered for sale.

Recognising that the basic economic purpose of private enterprise development is to raise the efficiency of a country's use of resources, development co–operation in the reform of the state enterprise sector should be guided by this technical consideration. The essential developmental purpose in some instances may best be served by a gradual reform starting with the termination of subsidies and the appointment of private management with performance–based remuneration, rather than by immediately converting a loss–making state monopoly into a private company whose new owners may be in a position to demand and get government guarantees of monopoly rights.

Development co–operation agencies should encourage a long–term approach to preparation of the conditions for the success of privatisation or commercialisation. For example, in less advanced countries, a regulatory framework may have to be created to ensure that the benefits of privatisation will be realised; an ad hoc alternative to a full–service financial market may be required to serve a large privatised enterprise; or a series of rationalisations may be necessary to make all or part of a state enterprise saleable.

The concern of labour unions and political leaders with the potential short–term unemployment effects of parastatal reform must be anticipated and constructively addressed by programmes of redeployment and training of workers who may be displaced. Aid may usefully be employed for this purpose.

j)   Enlarging Private Sector Provision of Social Services and Infrastructure

In advising and supporting developing countries in economic stabilisation and adjustment programmes, options should be examined for relief of budgetary pressures through privatisation of appropriate services (e.g., training, health or sanitation services) to the public. Whereas local private enterprise may have had no opportunity to demonstrate competence in a service historically monopolised by the state, a contract for a pilot project to produce and deliver such a service may be sufficient to induce a private company to initiate it. Development co–operation agencies, including investment finance and investment guarantee agencies, should consider supporting such pilot projects or providing technical advisers or helping to find foreign partners who can accelerate the development of local private capacity in such services. External agencies which retain a voice in the use of counterpart funds generated by their aid grants may nurture innovation by private companies by lending them seed capital or granting them technical consultancy funds.

National and foreign non–governmental organisations (NGOs) should be consulted in the search for private providers of social services or extenders of public services to remote areas.

II

A COMPENDIUM OF CURRENT PROGRAMMES

1. CO–OPERATION TO IMPROVE THE POLICY AND REGULATORY ENVIRONMENT IN DEVELOPING COUNTRIES

a) The Importance of Policies

Economic policies and regulations are crucial to private enterprise development. In setting, guiding or freeing prices, especially of foreign exchange, credit and wages, and in designing and administering taxation and protection of public interests, governments create the "environment" for enterprise and investment. Governmental policies and interventions that distort or frustrate markets have caused resources to flow into uneconomic or unproductive activity, and have led to the creation and support of unprofitable enterprises — enterprises that cannot compete on external markets without subsidy.

Regulation of economic life is a typical feature of developing countries' policies, as in exchange controls, administrative determination of exchange rates, interest rates and prices of basic consumption goods, rationing, controls on investment, import restrictions, allocations of credit and other controls. Regulations often extend beyond economic policies to impose a political design on the evolution of a sector or an entire national economy. Such controls, which usually are coupled with direct substitution of public for private initiative in various sectors of the economy, add to business uncertainties. Such regulations tend to discourage and restrict options for private investment and raise the costs of doing business.

National economic policies and controls that frustrate enterprise growth may be observed in four fields: trade, finance, competition, and labour markets.

    i) Trade. Import barriers stifle competition, encourage inefficient import–substitution, and limit access to new technologies, products and markets. High tariffs and quantitative restrictions promote and maintain monopolies. Overvalued exchange rates discourage local production by cheapening imports and make it difficult to export; in either case, the country's foreign exchange position suffers and it has less opportunity to develop economies of scale. Some countries exempt state enterprise from import duties, discouraging private competitors. Export taxes further reinforce anti–export bias in some countries.

17

ii) Finance. In most developing countries, private enterprises are handicapped by shortages of medium– and long–term credit and the virtual absence of organised markets for equity capital and debt finance. Commercial banks generally require heavy collateral, and their administrative costs are high. Credit, even at short term, is preferentially allocated to established clients. Public sector companies typically have disproportionate and preferential access to funds. Financial market regulations restrict small enterprises' access to organised credit. Small lenders' resources often are limited and subject to steady erosion because of low–interest policies and poor repayment records. Financial policies in some countries discourage the development of investment banks.

iii) Competition. Laws and judicial systems designed to nurture competition among enterprises are rare in developing countries. On the contrary, the state frequently sponsors monopolies, reserving economic activities for state companies. Private participation in mining, telecommunications, electric power and other services is commonly prohibited or circumscribed, depriving a developing country of the efficiencies that private enterprise might afford. State transit companies in many developing countries are protected from private competition, despite the efficiency of small private transit companies. Agricultural monopolies reduce farmer incentive and depress output.

iv) Labour. Labour law and practice handicap enterprise development in many countries. High social security charges, prohibitive penalties for laying off workers, and rigid collective bargaining rules frustrate new worker hirings and the use of part–time workers. Wage and bonus schemes are rarely linked to productivity or profitability, but are set under sector–wide or nationwide bargaining or administrative control. Regulations, together with official pressure to expand or maintain employment run up costs, weaken productivity, and damage competitiveness. Private firms cannot respond quickly to changing market conditions in the face of such rigidities.

b) External Support for Policy Reform

Growing recognition of the costs of inappropriate economic policies and excessive public intervention has led governments and development assistance agencies to co-operate in reform efforts in many developing countries. Such measures have ranged from freeing a single category of prices to comprehensive structural adjustment programmes, designed with the help of the International Monetary Fund and the World Bank.

Some DAC Members have helped developing countries make their infrastructure investments more supportive of productive enterprise. Donors have assisted in the review and revision of regulations and practices that frustrate private enterprise development, discourage exports, inhibit investment, or suppress competition. Many programmes seek to expand private sector access to credit. Some donors complement the major international financial institutions in helping developing countries avoid short–term adjustment problems when they liberalise imports, rationalise exchange rates, or reduce subsidies. For example, aid to Madagascar, Mali and Senegal helped these countries to restore fiscal order while carrying out adjustment programmes. Donors helped El Salvador, Egypt and Tanzania redesign their commercial and accounting laws and investment codes to encourage private investment. Bolivia undertook tax research and reform with donor help and Nigeria moved from a fixed to a floating exchange rate.

Multilateral Programmes

The World Bank has increasingly addressed policy issues affecting enterprise development. Through its policy dialogues and adjustment lending, the Bank seeks to improve the policy and regulatory environment of borrower countries. Its central theme is to rely more on markets and private enterprise and less on state controls. Structural and sectoral adjustment loans (SALs and SECALs) help developing countries minimise the costs of liberalisation measures that are required to stimulate local entrepreneurs and attract foreign investment. The Bank has expanded its adjustment lending; over the past five years policy–based lending has totalled 13 per cent of total lending, and a number of traditional projects now contain policy reform components. SALs in Pakistan and Dominica are designed to abolish, streamline, or liberalise investment regulations and procedures. Jamaica reduced red tape and stabilised its foreign exchange allocation system with World Bank help. Indonesia's trade policy adjustment loan facilitates more equal treatment between foreign and domestic investors. In Turkey SALs facilitated duty–free imports, made domestic credit more available, and enabled a review of mining, petroleum and tourism laws to promote foreign private investment.

Bilateral donors generally support the World Bank's structural and sectoral adjustment reforms, using policy framework papers (PFPs) to inform their work in developing countries. PFPs, prepared by countries requesting loans from the IMF's Structural Adjustment Facility with assistance from the IMF and World Bank, help identify priorities and provide a framework for policy reform. PFPs diagnose macroeconomic and structural problems, highlight the policies needed to address those problems, and set forth external financing needs. PFPs are being strengthened and made more specific, and efforts to involve bilateral donors are expanding. The objective is to avoid conflicting policy advice by donors, promote consistency, and facilitate structural reform.

To help certain recipient countries establish policies for adjustment and growth, and to avoid projects that frustrate policy reform, bilateral and multilateral agencies and recipients meet periodically in country–specific consultative groups (CG) and roundtables (RT), which are designed to co–ordinate aid in a way that promotes and reinforces policy reform in the participating recipient countries.

The World Bank sponsored the recent establishment of the *Multilateral Investment Guarantee Agency* (MIGA), which not only insures investors against non–commercial risks but fosters reforms of members' policies and procedures affecting foreign direct investment flows to and among developing countries.

The Foreign Investment Advisory Service (FIAS), a joint service of MIGA and the *International Finance Corporation* (IFC), helps developing–country governments structure their policies and institutions to attract productive foreign investment. Governments requesting help are not bound by FIAS recommendations, but since FIAS began operating in 1986 it has received an increasing number of requests for policy reform advice. FIAS also advises the World Bank on its efforts to help developing countries improve their economic, regulatory and institutional environments to attract foreign investment and encourage indigenous enterprises.

The *International Monetary Fund* (IMF) focuses on monetary, fiscal, and public investment issues. The IMF's special area of responsibility, exchange rate policy, is important in improving producer incentives, a key element in private enterprise development. The IMF Structural Adjustment Facility (SAF), which extends concessional resources to low–income countries undertaking adjustment programmes, is also important in setting the policy framework for private enterprise development. Market-determined exchange rates have been introduced in 17 Sub–Saharan African countries, and SAF support was provided to Bangladesh, Bolivia, Haiti and Nepal, among others. Many IMF programmes reflect close collaboration with the World Bank, as in Mauritius, where the government revised its investment code and abolished import licensing with help from the Bank and Fund.

The *United Nations Development Programme* (UNDP) supports public administration reforms and several specialised UN agencies in enterprise development. UNDP has also organized a series of regional consultative meetings and in–country workshops in which policy makers, corporate representatives, and officials from Chambers of Commerce and research institutes discuss how to improve the environment for private sector development.

The *OECD Business and Industry Advisory Committee* (BIAC) has suggested establishing trade and industry advisory panels composed of representatives from business, development agencies, local development banks, and other government agencies, to help host governments develop a better investment environment. These panels could monitor progress and report business opportunities to private investors from DAC countries.

Bilateral Programmes

Policy dialogue is an essential element in *United States* aid strategy. The US Agency for International Development (AID) has increased efforts to help developing countries make their economies more attractive to potential investors by focusing assistance on measures to improve developing countries' environment for private enterprise. In Bolivia, Ecuador and Haiti, AID–sponsored studies laid the basis for tax reform. El Salvador rewrote its export law, and Mali revised its commercial code and relaxed price controls with AID assistance. Policy dialogue helped bring about more appropriate exchange rate policies in Costa Rica and Guatemala. In Bangladesh AID is working with the government to rationalise interest rates, mobilise savings, and improve financial institutions. In Gambia, AID helped the government abolish its rice and fertilizer monopoly. Private merchants now import rice, and fertilizer is being sold to private traders at market prices. In Mali AID and other donors are helping the government liberalise the cereals market, reduce consumer subsidies, and improve producer incentives.

US AID has made tax reform an integral part of policy dialogue. AID encourages developing countries to change restrictive tax laws and adopt policies that provide a suitable tax environment for financial markets development. Among the measures encouraged are lowering the explicit and implicit taxes imposed on financial intermediaries and adopting lower marginal tax rates for corporations. The tax reform legislation in Jamaica and Grenada, which reduced high marginal tax rates and removed disincentives to productive investment, is based upon extensive research supported by AID. In Guatemala and the Dominican Republic, AID is working to help reduce tax rates on export earnings and increase incentives for exporting. Tax reform is an important feature of AID's private sector development programme in Senegal.

The *United Kingdom* provides experts and consultants to host countries requesting advice on foreign direct investment. Britain has actively supported structural adjustment programmes undertaken by Sub–Saharan African countries in agreement with the IMF/IBRD. British technical co–operation also promotes and assists structural adjustment reforms.

Germany supports developing countries' economic and social policy reforms and structural adjustment efforts through policy dialogue, programme assistance, and cofinancing arrangements with the World Bank's International Development Association (IDA). Germany's programme aid, which accounts for a substantial portion of its bilateral ODA commitments, have promoted policy reform and structural adjustment in many developing countries.

2. INSTITUTIONAL SUPPORT FOR PRIVATE ENTERPRISE DEVELOPMENT

Structural adjustment creates new business opportunities. Devaluation has made exporting more profitable, trade liberalisation has made it easier to import production inputs and to export goods, and deregulation has created a freer business environment. Still, the evolution of diversified, viable enterprises, particularly in the less developed countries, requires more than a favourable climate for business. Dependable infrastructure, adaptable human resources, and a financial system that efficiently mobilises and allocates credit are also essential.

By identifying institutional and human impediments to enterprise development and assisting developing countries to carry out programmes to correct these deficiencies, aid agencies can make important contributions to the stimulation of private enterprise.

Some of the assistance required in private sector development is an adaptation of familiar activities. For example, donors have assisted in revising procurement and credit procedures so that private firms have greater access to external credit lines; prepared and disseminated feasibility studies and market surveys to local firms; given financial and technical support to export promotion agencies; provided technical, managerial, and marketing assistance to local enterprises; assisted in the transfer and adaptation of technology to local businesses; provided vocational and managerial training to local entrepreneurs; and developed grass roots assistance networks for micro–enterprises.

a) Financial Assistance through Local Development Banks

Local development banks, or development finance institutions (DFIs), have been central and essential to the private sector in developing countries. They have played a unique role in channelling funds from multilateral and bilateral lenders to selected industries. Their performance, however, is now being re–examined. Many DFIs suffer from government interference in lending decisions, weak management, over–dependence on donors, and insufficient capacity to mobilise funds. Artificially low interest rates, poor credit allocation, and over–investment in uncompetitive industries have also marred some DFIs.

21

Nevertheless, DFI lending will continue in the absence of a better alternative. The *World Bank* plans to continue using DFIs to channel assistance to developing–country businesses. The World Bank estimates that over the past five years about 25 per cent of Bank and IDA lending provided direct support to the private sector through DFIs and commercial banks. The *IFC* reports that DFIs have mobilised over $40 billion in developing countries and created over 2.5 million jobs. *BIAC* has recommended that DFIs widen their scope to include medium– and large–scale manufacturing enterprises. BIAC has also suggested that DFIs compile and distribute to potential investors a guide on incentives, support measures, and industrial development programmes in select host countries.

Several *DAC Member countries* and the *European Economic Community* provide financial support to local enterprises through development banks or commercial banks. The *IFC* has extended equity finance through local banks. More information on IFC's role may be found on page 28.

The *European Economic Community* finances projects in African, Caribbean, and Pacific (ACP) countries either out of the European Development Fund (EDF), usually via special loans (Lomé III provides 600 million ECU for this purpose, at 40 years, 10–year grace period, interest rate reduced from 1 per cent to 0.5 per cent for the least developed countries), or by loans from the European Investment Bank (EIB). EIB has a special mandate to assist industry, agro–industry, tourism and mining, and energy, transport and telecommunications. These EIB loans are accompanied by EDF interest rate subsidies, granted directly to enterprises or through local development banks.

US AID works with local development institutions to provide financial assistance to private enterprises. In the Dominican Republic, for example, AID supports a private development foundation that makes loans to micro–entrepreneurs. Since 1983, AID funds have helped establish seven new banks to finance non–traditional exports in Latin America and the Caribbean. One such institution is the Trafalgar Development Bank in Jamaica, which was established in 1984. It provides medium– and long–term credit to small and medium–sized enterprises. Over 40 loans have been made in agro–industry, fishing, furniture manufacturing, data entry, electronics and other export industries.

In *Germany*, the Federal Ministry for Economic Co–operation through the Kreditanstalt fuer Wiederaufbau (KfW) extends financial assistance to local development banks for small and medium–sized enterprises (SMEs), particularly in the industrial and agricultural sectors. For 25 years, the KfW has co–operated with some 90 local credit institutions in more than 50 developing countries, accounting for about 10 per cent of all its financial co–operation transactions. Cumulative commitments in this sector total about $3.3 billion. At the end of 1987 commitments by the German Finance Company for Investments in Developing Countries (DEG) to 61 development banks in developing countries totalled about DM 331 million (of which about DM 130 million were funds–in–trust). The DEG made development funds available in Africa to 33 local banks and funds and regional institutions; in Asia to 16 local institutions; in Central and South America to two regional institutions and six local banks; and in Southern Europe to one local development bank. The DEG also participated in funding venture capital companies in Argentina, Bangladesh, Côte d'Ivoire, Israel, Korea, and Malawi. In Kenya the DEG has begun two pilot projects. One is a special development company for small enterprises and artisans. The other is a fund which makes equity capital available for the rehabilitation of private small and medium–sized enterprises.

Japan has launched a new scheme for financial co–operation with the six member countries of the Association of South East Asian Nations (ASEAN): Brunei, Indonesia, Malaysia, the Philippines, Singapore and Thailand. The $2 billion ASEAN/Japan Development Fund will provide untied loans, partly on Overseas Development Assistance (ODA) terms, to support private sector development, promote economic co–operation between ASEAN countries, and encourage Japanese investors to establish joint ventures there. The loans will be committed over a three–year period for projects or programmes selected jointly by Japan and ASEAN, or by individual ASEAN member countries. The Fund will be constituted from public and private sources in Japan, and will be added to existing financial co–operation. ODA loans provided by the Fund will be administered by the Overseas Economic Co-operation Fund and will benefit recipients that are at present eligible for ODA loans. The interest rate for these special ODA loans will be reduced to 2.5 per cent from the current 3 per cent. Commercial loans to be committed by the Fund will be administered by Japan's Export–Import Bank and will possibly carry more favourable terms than ordinary EXIM Bank loans.

Switzerland has worked with local development banks in a number of assistance programmes to agriculture and industry, particularly small and medium–sized enterprises in the form of grants or loans (India, Madagascar, Rwanda, etc.). In the area of trade and financial policy, the projects carried out by the International Trade Centre and financed by Switzerland provide technical assistance to many local finance institutions. Currently there are plans for a major project, which would be financed jointly with UNDP, involving more than 50 development finance institutions.

b) Direct Assistance to Small and Medium–Sized Enterprises

Small and medium–sized enterprises (SMEs) providing local goods and services help poor countries grow. While very small businesses create jobs with relatively little capital, they are not always more labour–intensive. Still, they form the backbone of developing country commerce and industry and are well–suited to local technologies and resources. SMEs are handicapped in some countries by industrialisation policies favouring large, often state–owned, enterprises and by other unfavourable policies and regulations. For example, duty–free capital imports and artificially high exchange rates favour large, capital–intensive businesses. Credit is a problem. SMEs have difficulty borrowing from local banks. Restrictive banking laws combined with low, sometimes negative, real interest rates prevent banks from recovering the high costs of SME lending. Some laws require collateral of up to 150 per cent of the loan. Minimum wage requirements, statutory firing limits, and social security laws also retard SMEs.

Without effective technical, managerial, and marketing skills, SMEs are not likely to raise productivity, diversify products, and expand their businesses. Some donors are trying to provide technical assistance to small entrepreneurs, directly or through intermediaries, as well as helping to improve the policy environment for SMEs. Management development centres and business advisory services can help SMEs raise their productivity and marketing. Local advisory networks are helping SMEs with specific problems.

The *Inter–American Development Bank* finances small projects in the least developed parts of Latin America. The small projects programme provides to local businesses, co–operatives, and similar entities low–cost loans of up to $500 000 per project (local currency repayable) and a maximum of $250 000 for technical assistance grants. The Bank's loan and technical co–operation operations in low–income countries, including pre–investment facilities, also benefit indigenous entrepreneurs. The Bank's new affiliate, the *Inter–American Investment Corporation*, is focusing on private small and medium–scale enterprises.

The *Asian Development Bank* lends to small and medium–sized enterprises through governments, local financial institutions, or directly. Since 1986, the Bank has been authorized to make loans to private borrowers without their government's guarantee. The new programme is expected to enlarge enterprises' access to domestic and external finance. Since 1982, the Bank has been authorised to take equity participations in certain types of private enterprise.

Germany, the *Netherlands* and *Sweden* are launching partnerships between their commercial banks and local banks which specialise in small–scale lending. The purpose is to extend credit to small entrepreneurs, farmers and small–scale agro-industries which normally have little access to credit.

The *Netherlands* supports industrial service centres in developing countries which reduce entrepreneurs' overhead costs by grouping them under one roof.

The *United States'* Agency for International Development (AID) has relied upon private financial institutions, co–operatives, and private voluntary organisations to provide credit to medium, small and micro–entrepreneurs. US AID provides direct loans and loan guarantees, and introduces small businesses to banks and other commercial lenders. The Private Enterprise Revolving Fund extends loans to developing countries' private financial institutions and to individual enterprises that do not normally have access to credit. In Indonesia, an AID project is developing credit programmes to mobilise local savings. Loans range from $50 to $500, principally for short–term working capital for small traders. In Cameroon, an AID project is providing members of the Co–operative Credit Union League with training in financial management, savings promotion, and credit administration. Credit programmes include non–farm credit as well as small farmer production credit. This self–supporting league has over 60 000 members and has made loans valued at over $15 million.

Canada's International Development Agency (CIDA) and International Development Research Centre support financial and technical assistance and small business training in developing countries. Canada has set up with the World Bank's International Finance Corporation a trust fund to finance technical assistance activities in developing countries. Bilateral efforts are complemented by Canadian NGOs working in small enterprise development.

Several programmes are in place, including credit schemes which enable women to become independent wage earners. The role of women in small enterprise development often poses special problems. Women generally have a weaker labour market position than men, although working conditions, job tenure and the power to organise vary from country to country. Special efforts are required with respect to labour legislation, social policies, education and health care to ensure that economic development provides more equitable conditions for women.

The *German* Government's Integrated Experts Programme enables private entrepreneurs in developing countries to obtain advisory services from German experts on the basis of the local pay scale. The German Government will top up the experts' salaries if their activities have particular significance to development (introduction of new technologies, off–plant training, etc.).

c)   Special Programmes for Micro–Enterprises

Micro–enterprises (MEs) employ the poor in a wide range of productive activities. They typically consist of two or three people — often family members — who engage in agriculture, handicrafts, trading, services, or manufacturing. MEs could play a greater role with more credit, but official credit generally goes to larger enterprises, even though practical experience has shown that it is possible to lend profitably and effectively to MEs. Small, private, local lenders exerting community pressure on defaulters lend successfully to MEs in a number of developing countries. Internal, community–based lending networks can provide start–up capital for small entrepreneurs, but as these businesses grow they must normally rely on larger institutions for new credit.

Labour–intensive businesses using local resources to employ workers outside the modern sector constitute a formidable economic force. MEs make up the bulk of the private sector in many developing countries. In Peru it is estimated that MEs generate one–third of GDP and employ 60 per cent of the active population.

A number of researchers have found that small, especially very small firms may not use resources more efficiently than larger firms, nor are they reliably more labour–intensive. Their performance varies between industries and countries. The investment cost per job of some small enterprises in West Africa, for example, is two or three times higher than in parts of Asia. Micro–entrepreneurs also have limited incentive to save and invest, and usually remain on the economy's fringes. That these issues raise questions about the extent to which MEs should be promoted does not diminish the value of MEs. They are typically very competitive in producing a limited range of goods unsuited to large–scale, capital–intensive production. Domestic raw materials insufficient for large operations will often suffice for small ones. Informal investments frequently have higher rates of return than those in the modern sector, and MEs are often the only private options in an overregulated economy. MEs require little capital and can adjust rapidly to local demand.

A number of specialised credit institutions try to help small businessmen with finance and technical assistance, but these programmes traditionally lend to enterprises employing at least 50 people. Smaller businesses get very little of the credit reserved for the medium–sized and small businesses, and MEs (less than ten people) rarely get any medium– or long–term finance from the official financial market.

Micro–enterprise support also helps women to participate in development. The small–scale entrepreneurial efforts of women can be enhanced by special measures which are adapted to their levels of training and literacy.

A number of community–based lenders are extending credit, usually without collateral, to borrowers in such countries as Bangladesh, Zaire and Malaysia. Since 1983 *Bangladesh's Grameen Bank* has helped 630 000 persons in over 14 000 villages set up over 500 different types of business. Grameen claims a 98 per cent repayment rate and also turns a profit, employing 4 000 staff members who lend $1 million a month to landless peasants. Loans average $60 at 16 per cent interest. Eighty per cent of the borrowers are women. The Grameen system is based on peer support and peer pressure and on close contact between bank and borrower. Villagers meet weekly with a Grameen representative to discuss business and monitor loan repayments. Borrowers may pool their resources to invest in larger ventures. Loans have been used to make furniture, baskets, fish nets and farm implements. Borrowers raise fruit, cotton, sugar cane and vegetables with seeds provided by the bank. Grameen has received and repaid a $37 million loan from the International Fund for Agricultural Development (IFAD), and expects another $125 million from IFAD. Malaysia started a similar programme in 1985, and non–profit groups in Indonesia hope to duplicate Grameen's success. Rwanda, Egypt, Kenya and Sudan are also considering Grameen–style lending systems.

Mali's $9 million *Village Development Fund* enjoys a 100 per cent repayment rate. The four year–old programme has provided 3 000 farmers in 85 villages with over $1 million, enabling them to buy tools, fertilizers and animals. Like Grameen, borrowers are subject to strict repayment criteria: their village must approve every loan, and it is responsible for repayments. Loan–seeking communities must put down 10 per cent of the amount they wish to borrow, and borrowers are charged annual interest rates of 9 per cent, with repayments due over five years. Like Grameen, Mali's Village Development Fund receives IFAD support.

Cameroon's tontines also provide capital to small entrepreneurs, although the loans are normally larger than Grameen's. Like the Grameen Bank and the Village Development Fund, peer pressure discourages delinquency, and low overheads enable the tontines to set lower rates than the banks. Tontines generally consist of homogeneous groups from the same ethnic background, workplace or neighbourhood, who meet monthly to contribute a fixed share to a community pool of funds. The tontine pool is rotated among eligible members to expand a business or make new investments. Delinquent participants are rejected by the community and have difficulty joining another tontine. The tontine system operates in Burkina Faso, Ghana, Zaire and Rwanda.

The *United States* AID Missions support micro–enterprise as the principal focus of private sector development projects or as micro–components of health, nutrition, rural development, or agribusiness projects. Projects focus on private and voluntary organisations, co–operatives, national development foundations, credit unions, small business associations, and intermediate financial institutions. Examples of activities include the Dominican Republic, where AID contributes to a private development foundation that makes loans to small entrepreneurs. AID also supports six technical assistance centres there that help very small businesses increase management and business skills. In Bangladesh, AID supports a micro–industries development service. And in Jamaica, AID support to the National Development Foundation has resulted in the creation of over more than 5 600 jobs.

AID's Bureau for Science and Technology develops programmes to support the design, implementation, and evaluation of micro–enterprise projects. Its ARIES Project (Assistance to Resource Institutions for Enterprise Support) provides research, training, and technical assistance to AID Missions. ARIES engages in case studies and distributes training materials on credit programmes, financial intermediaries, enterprise strategy, and staff training. ARIES also helps to strengthen local business organisations which assist micro–entrepreneurs in local communities, and serves as a vehicle for US AID missions to compare experience. ARIES has carried out assignments in over 20 countries, including Bangladesh, Ecuador, El Salvador, Honduras, Indonesia, Jordan, Somalia, Thailand, Zaire, and Zambia.

The *German* Government has recognised the importance of micro–enterprise development and has started a pilot programme, "New Business Creation", for potential entrepreneurs. This programme includes training, on–the–spot advice, and support services. Its most distinctive feature is that the training courses encourage pragmatic business decision–making. The programme was tested with considerable success in Nepal, and the scheme will be introduced in other developing countries.

d) Official Support for the Transfer and Adaptation of Technology

Canada's, International Development Agency provides incentives to Canadian industry for the establishment of joint ventures and adaptation of modern technology in developing countries.

US AID has worked to overcome the absence of modern, appropriate technology in developing countries in several ways. First, AID encourages policies that promote technology transfer and adaptation. Such policies include investment codes that are fair to investors, protection of intellectual property rights, and product standards codes. Second, AID supports intermediaries that are competent in technology transfer and development, such as Appropriate Technology International (ATI). AID also uses joint ventures as a way of transferring technology and increasing trade. An AID project in India, the Programme for the Advancement of Commercial Technology (PACT), finances research in product adaptation, especially by joint ventures, for import or export between the United States and India. Finally, AID supports country-specific projects that promote technology transfer and adaptation. In Nepal AID has supported field testing of various appropriate technologies. Private entrepreneurs are involved in manufacturing and marketing biogas units, grain storage bins, water turbines, irrigation pumps, and other technologies. Privately-owned stores are being established to sell and service locally manufactured technology.

The *German* Government operates through KfW a special programme to promote investments of German small and medium-scale firms in developing countries. KfW extends loans to German firms at 3.5 per cent interest (for relending in developing countries at 2.5 per cent interest) with a 15-year maturity (including five-year grace) and a ceiling of 2.5 million DM (about $1.3 million) per loan, covering up to 50 per cent of the investment value. KfW also finances up to 50 per cent of the costs of feasibility studies; if the studies have a negative result or if the investment cannot be made for reasons beyond the responsibility of the investor, then repayment of the loans may be postponed. An accompanying "technology programme" finances up to 50 per cent of the costs which German small or medium-scale firms incur in transferring "new" technology. An enterprise may obtain a loan of up to 2.5 million DM (about $1.3 million) from 1 to 2.5 per cent interest over 15 years.

The *Swiss* Government financially supports technology fairs in Geneva, Mexico and Manila. These fairs match developing countries seeking private investment with Swiss companies that want to sell technologies to companies in developing countries. Contributions to this programme have been renewed for three years. The scheme is now limited to seven Asian countries: Pakistan, Nepal, Bangladesh, Sri Lanka, Thailand, Indonesia and the Philippines. The Swiss Government also provides financial support for the promotion of joint ventures and the transfer of technology to developing countries. In addition, representatives from investment promotion agencies in several developing countries are invited to spend up to a year in Switzerland to try and interest Swiss firms in investing in their countries.

The "Sister-Industry" programme encourages *Swedish* enterprises to enter into long-term technology transfer contracts with counterpart enterprises in developing countries and to extend home-country training in production, management and marketing. The Swedish Government subsidises part of the costs. The Swedish National Board for Technical Development supports Swedish enterprises in adapting products and techniques for export to developing countries.

The *Netherlands* provides official financing for in–plant training for sister industries in developing countries. Aid funds can also be applied directly to technical assistance to private companies, especially for institutional development.

e) Private Sector Vocational Training

Some Member governments finance training in book–keeping, auditing, commercial law, marketing and management. *BIAC* has underlined the value of in–house training that private firms could offer if properly reimbursed.

The *Swedish* Institute of Management trains private businessmen and public administrators in developing countries through the Applied International Management Programme.

German technical assistance is used to assist German companies in running in–plant training programmes for skilled workers and low and middle–level management in developing countries. Firms providing training under this programme can claim a subsidy of $40 to $160 per trainee each month. Preference is given to small and medium–sized firms, but *BIAC* has suggested that this programme's impact could be enhanced if it were broadened to include large German and foreign companies. Training programmes for private sector employees in developing countries have been expanded considerably. Managers, engineers, and senior technicians are upgrading their qualifications to achieve more efficient production and better products. Beneficiaries include Pakistan leather garment industries, wood and rattan furniture industries in Malaysia, Indonesia and the Philippines, and food processing industries in Latin America. Under a comprehensive scheme executed by a German NGO and the associations of industry in five Latin American countries, more than 500 production managers have received advanced professional training.

The *United States* sponsors Entrepreneurs International, which brings entrepreneurs from developing countries to the United States for on–the–job training. In Costa Rica, US AID is financing a programme which trains managers in the private sector, the financial system, and universities. To date, 3 500 private sector participants have been trained in areas such as general management, production management, and export promotion and marketing. In Mali, a joint Peace Corps/AID project teaches basic business skills to small–scale enterprise employees.

Canada has created within CIDA a facility to support management training institutions in Canada. Three institutions have been established, with Canadian industrialists providing management training in such fields as civil aviation, telecommunications, and large projects.

Switzerland's vocational training programmes target institutions in developing countries and basic training. Increasingly these programmes focus on direct training in firms and business management. Assistance to the informal sector in the Sahel countries, and in Rwanda, India and Bangladesh, regularly includes a training element.

f) Promotional Role of the International Finance Corporation

The *International Finance Corporation* (IFC) contributes to local enterprise development, devoting about one–third of its staff to these activities. IFC lends and invests in private companies in developing countries. At the end of 1987 IFC's portfolio included financial stakes in 404 companies in 77 countries. IFC complements its lending with policy and financial advisory services to increase enterprise efficiency. By introducing new managerial and financing techniques IFC helps to restructure and revitalise declining enterprises. Services include sectoral policy advice, technical assistance, and training and support.

The *IFC* seeks to serve local enterprises' financial needs through long–term finance. Equipment finance is made available by IFC–supported leasing companies, and special programmes are set up with commercial banks to provide small and medium–sized enterprises (SMEs) with longer–term loans and business advisory services. IFC promotes local venture capital funds capable of raising equity capital for SMEs. It also has recruited and supervised small business advisors in Kenya, Sri Lanka, and Thailand. IFC advisers helped reorganise commercial banks in Indonesia and Sri Lanka, and IFC has undertaken project work in Kenya, Sri Lanka, Thailand, the Dominican Republic, Malawi, the Philippines, and Cameroon. The IFC's Caribbean Project Development Facility (CPDF) helps small entrepreneurs prepare and develop projects for financing. Sectors include agriculture, light industry and tourism. The African counterpart of the CPDF, the African Project Development Facility (APDF), was set up in late 1986, and demand for its services has been strong: over 400 requests for assistance have been received, out of which about 100 business men are expected to be helped during the facility's initial four years.

The IFC has also established an Emerging Markets Fund of about $1 billion with contributions from the Japanese private sector. The Fund invests in businesses in Asia and Latin America through their stock markets. An African Management Services Company (AMSCo) has also recently begun operations. AMSCo identifies senior business executives to work with African companies and train local managers. Countries where initial AMSCo services are being provided include Cameroon, Côte d'Ivoire and Zimbabwe.

g) Other Promotional Measures

The *Canadian* Government supports business councils in countries such as India, Pakistan, China and Egypt, and sponsors missions to identify business opportunities in host countries.

In *France*, the Directorate for Scientific and Technical Co–operation for Development (DCSTD) is trying to strengthen private enterprise in developing countries through diplomatic missions (or, in the case of the Maghreb countries, through the Caisse centrale de coopération économique). The French Department for Relations with Enterprises administers a special fund for reimbursable feasibility studies. Aid is also extended for innovative projects — including small credits — and cofinancing is undertaken with the EEC Centre for Industrial Development in Brussels.

The *German* Government has developed a trade fair promotion programme for developing countries. This programme is administered by the German Agency for Technical Cooperation (GTZ), which provides consultancy services on product design and marketing as well as grants for the participation of private firms from developing countries at international trade fairs. Beyond the scope of GTZ's PROTRADE programme, there is also an intention to assist developing country producers directly, through private trading companies, in improving product quality and marketing. GTZ consultancy services have been extended to cover not only consumer goods but also technical packaging. To promote trade among the developing countries, advisory services are offered to trade fair and exhibition agencies in developing countries. GTZ co-operates with other trade promotion agencies in Europe and with the EEC's COLEACP, the special agricultural and horticultural export promotion agency for the ACP Member countries in Africa, the Caribbean and the Pacific.

The *German Programme for the Promotion of Business Cooperation* (BC Programme) offers advisory services for industry in developing countries to promote trade, technology transfer and joint ventures between German businesses and those in Africa, Asia, and Latin America. This programme may be expanded to cover production and marketing services. Policy questions and institutional problems in chambers of commerce and export councils may also be included.

The *Swiss* Government has established information and consultancy services for developing countries through the Office suisse d'expansion commerciale (OSEC) in Lausanne. OSEC advises developing country exporters on the Swiss market, briefs Swiss importers on export tenders from developing countries, and establishes direct contacts between trading partners. The Swiss Government has also financed the participation of four developing countries (Egypt, Senegal, Côte d'Ivoire and Peru) in the Swiss Samples Fair and the Comptoir suisse.

Examples of literature containing practical advice for enterprises in developing countries include a *German* manual, "German Enterprises and Developing Countries", and a *Swedish* publication, "Improve your Business". A *Danish* government agency published a brochure listing potential joint venture partners in developing countries.

The *United States* AID supports the International Executive Service Corps (IESC), and several other DAC Members support similar agencies that assign volunteer businessmen to give short-term management assistance to businesses in developing countries.

US AID, the German aid programme, and a number of other donors also help business and trade associations in developing countries present their views to government. US AID Missions in developing countries often solicit local private sector views to ensure that policy changes are responsive to the needs of the private sector. In some countries, AID relies on business associations to provide training and other services. In Jamaica, US AID's support to the Private Sector Organization of Jamaica has enabled that group to be an effective voice for change in economic and regulatory policies. In Jordan, AID cofinances services to entrepreneurs through the Chamber of Industry. Germany arranges collaboration between German business associations and counterparts in developing countries.

3. STRENGTHENING DOMESTIC CAPITAL MARKETS

Sound financial markets foster robust private enterprises and economic growth. Banks, other savings institutions, and securities markets expand the supply of available funds for investment and business. Equity markets allocate capital to activities yielding good returns, broaden the range of investment opportunities for investors, and moderate dependence on debt finance. Business and investment opportunities depend largely upon entrepreneurs' access to domestic sources of capital; hence the development of an open market. Accessible financial institutions are a major feature of national development. Without a strong domestic financial market, privatisation is difficult and economic efficiency suffers. Financial market constraints also frustrate private and foreign investors.

Despite the obvious advantages of a strong domestic capital market, conditions and policies in developing countries often constrain financial sector development. Regulations and tax laws frequently favour lending and borrowing over equity finance. For example, most governments tax dividends at higher rates than interest, and make borrowers' interest expenses tax–deductible. This pushes savings into debt instruments, encourages debt financing, and contributes to over–indebtedness in many developing countries. Protected enterprises also constrain financial sectors. Oligopolies are sheltered from competitive pressures and business disclosure requirements; majority shareholders — often families — are not subject to pressure by stockholders. As long as potential shareholders feel that majority owners are exempt from competitive pressures, a large and efficient equity market is not likely to emerge. Pension funds, insurance companies, and mutual funds, which are major mobilisers and allocators of savings in developed countries, are typically frail or non–existent in less developed countries. In order to attract foreign investment in the capital markets of developing countries, governments must adopt international accounting standards and practices that ensure investor protection.

The International Finance Corporation (IFC) has had the leading role as adviser and investor in developing countries' capital markets, and in developing their access to foreign sources of private funds. Mobilising domestic savings requires sound fiscal, monetary and investor–protection policies, and IFC has assisted more than 70 governments in designing appropriate legal and fiscal frameworks and in training managers and technical staffs of financial institutions. In promoting foreign portfolio investment in developing countries, IFC has advised Member governments on legislation, tax laws, financial regulations, and investor protection policies. IFC helped write India's securities law and train the manager of its stock exchange. The Corporation also helped computerise India's stock exchange and assisted in establishing an Indian rating agency. IFC was the lead manager of a $50 million note issue for the Latin American Export Bank, providing the first new money from the international capital markets for a private Latin American company since the debt crisis started in 1982. IFC has also acted as the lead manager of the public offering of the Thailand Fund, and as co–lead manager of the offering of the Malaysia Fund. IFC also promotes and invests in specialised financial institutions such as brokerage and money market houses, investment, export and merchant banks, and leasing and insurance companies. This investment has covered over 67 financial institutions in some 34 developing countries.

The top five "emerging" capital markets of developing countries (Brazil, India, Korea, Malaysia, Taiwan) are now comparable in size to a typical national market in Europe, and by the end of 1985 foreign investment in them exceeded $1 billion. Other markets have fared well too. Jordan's market, established only in 1978, has over 100 listings with a total capitalisation of $3 billion, and investors do not have to pay withholding taxes on dividends or capital gains. Nigeria's market had reached a capitalisation of $3.8 billion by 1986 with 94 listed stocks, and there are plans to open up the market to international investors.

The *United States* AID is trying to promote integrated financial markets and competitive financial institutions and policies. Its objective is to foster markets that mobilise private savings, allocate savings to investments yielding maximum returns, and increase the participation of the general populace. To this end, AID has provided technical assistance, training, and credit to: *a)* support and improve development finance institutions; *b)* help existing banks add long–term lending to their traditional short–term lending operations; c) increase the supply of credit to business; and d) eliminate impediments to capital movement among regions or sectors. AID also encourages developing countries to develop and use new forms of debt and equity instruments.

AID's Bureau for Programme and Policy Co–ordination has issued a policy paper on financial markets development, covering macroeconomic policy reform, mobilization of domestic savings, credit allocation policies, legal and regulatory constraints, tax policies, informal financial markets, credit policy, financial training and standards, and new financial instruments and institutions.

AID's Bureau for Private Enterprise has designed new investment concepts, instruments, and approaches for mobilisation of investment capital in developing countries and through international financial markets. These include tapping international sources of private venture capital, using blocked funds, debt/equity conversion, and credit enhancement through securitisation. AID Missions in Kenya and Indonesia are providing assistance to help improve their stock markets.

4. TRADE AND EXPORT PROMOTION

International trade offers many enterprises opportunities for growth and challenges to productive efficiency. Export promotion is therefore an integral feature of private enterprise development programmes.

Aid agencies have assisted trade promotion centres and other institutions responsible for export development by training staff, and by funding feasibility studies and business development funds. Several DAC Members have established import promotion centres and organised trade fairs to encourage imports from developing countries. All of these efforts have helped to expand developing countries' exports, but adverse economic policies have often limited export gains.

Inward–looking policies, especially protection of uncompetitive domestic producers against import competition, combined with overvalued exchange rates, have been common impediments to export expansion. The most successful export programmes have focused on removing these constraints. By advising and financing governments to adjust to an outward–oriented policy framework, donors have helped some developing countries expand and diversify their exports. The World Bank and IMF have played the lead role in policy reform, with bilateral donors generally providing technical and institutional assistance, and, in an increasing number of countries, import financing to execute orderly liberalisation.

Although trade performance depends mainly on policies conducive to enterprise growth, effective export development also requires a supportive institutional framework. DAC Members have set up programmes to help developing countries build their export capacity through expert advice, training, and in some cases budgetary support.

Japan has assigned its successful Japan External Trade Organization (JETRO) the new mission of assisting developing countries to adapt their exports to the quality and design preferences of the Japanese market, and to improve their marketing methods there.

Canada has set up a Trade Facilitation Office, funded by CIDA, to provide developing countries with practical assistance through market information, trade seminars, and training materials.

The *Finnish* Development Co-operation Programme runs training courses and seminars, both on its own and with the International Trade Centre in Geneva. Since 1969, this programme has arranged an annual course on trade promotion and export marketing. More than 250 senior managers and officials, mainly from African and other low-income countries have participated in 14 courses. In addition, courses and seminars have been held in product design and adaptation, packaging technology, import management, contracting, and administration.

The *German* Government has developed a trade fair promotion programme for developing countries. The Association of German Wholesale and Foreign Trade has set up a liaison office to promote imports from developing countries. This office helps to market products from developing countries and assists German business in establishing contacts there.

The *Netherlands* helps export promotion centres in Bangladesh, Egypt and the ASEAN countries to open trade offices in the Netherlands. It also extends bilateral assistance for market research and training to the national export promotion institutions in Indonesia and Egypt.

Norway provides training and marketing programmes for several developing countries.

Sweden is a major supporter of the UNCTAD/GATT International Trade Centre, which promotes trade between developed and developing-countries. Sweden's Import Promotion Office facilitates imports from developing country partners. Sweden's Generalised System of Programmes (GSP) covers a wide range of agricultural and industrial products from developing countries, and has no quotas, ceilings, or duties.

The *United Kingdom's* Trade Agency aids low-income countries by financing trade information services and trade visits. This work is supported by the Tropical Products Institute. The UK also finances an eight-week training course at Manchester University for trade officials from developing countries.

The *United States* AID tries to accelerate export-led growth in developing countries by several means. At the policy level, AID is encouraging recipients of large-scale non-project import financing to introduce more flexibility into their exchange rate regimes, reduce export-impeding policies such as excessive foreign exchange controls and import restrictions, and reduce protection for import-competing industries. AID attaches conditions consistent with those of the World Bank in some of its assistance to economic stabilisation or structural adjustment programmes, including liberalisation of import controls and reduction of export restrictions. AID also designs some of its import-financing assistance to give priority to imports used as production inputs in export-oriented industries.

AID's efforts to promote export expansion and diversification by developing countries have been especially extensive in Central America and the Caribbean, where these economies are taking advantage of trade opportunties offered by the US "Caribbean Basin Initiative". AID projects focus on training and technical assistance, and on encouraging private foreign investment in export-oriented businesses. With technical assistance and local currency support, free zone industrial parks have been established throughout the Caribbean basin to facilitate export manufacturing and assembly. These zones have helped generate employment and diversify production.

Under AID's Market and Technology Access Project, commercial intermediaries are used to promote trade and investment between American and local firms.

Effective support for Indonesian exports is being provided by specialised joint ventures between several major *Japanese* trading companies and Indonesian manufacturers. The Japanese companies provide technical advice and in some instances short-term credit to assist Indonesian producers to compete in overseas markets.

Export development also includes vocational training, management, standardization, product design and quality control, etc., as well as practical training in enterprises of DAC Member countries. Training activities are most effective when they focus on practical problems at the enterprise level and take into account a country's specific circumstances. The logistics of the export marketing process, i.e., the chain of production, transportation, marketing and distribution, are essential to successful export development programmes.

5. TECHNICAL AND FINANCIAL ASSISTANCE FOR THE RATIONALISATION OR DIVESTITURE OF STATE ENTERPRISES

Successful privatisation involves more than simply selling shares in a nationalised industry, and successful rationalisation or commercialisation of an enterprise involves more than denying it budget subsidies. The scope for enhancing efficiency through rationalisation or privatisation of state enterprises is limited by the extent to which markets can be made more competitive. This commonly requires liberalisation of controls on prices and investments, the removal of market restrictions, subsidies and other supports of monopoly, and — more difficult — the actual emergence of competition in the market.

Privatisation in developing countries has been slow. Governments often have difficulty finding buyers when they attempt divestitures. Privatisation is delayed in some cases by the same political and economic factors that contributed to the state enterprises' inefficiency: non-economic mandates from governments; the obligation to hire and retain staff in excess of operating requirements; the obligation to provide a market for certain crops or supplies of certain goods at non-market prices, etc. The lack of private capital or interested entrepreneurs which caused government to resort to state intervention in the first place continues to limit the possibilities of privatisation even now, especially in the less developed countries. The undeveloped state of formal capital markets makes public share offerings difficult. Lack of confidence in governments' new faith in market economics may deter both foreign and domestic investors. From the point of view of governments, the cost of forcing thousands of redundant employees out of work are major deterents to both privatisation and commercialisation.

Several *DAC Members* and *multilateral institutions* provide financial and technical assistance to governments undertaking programmes to rationalise parastatals. Development agencies facilitate privatisation by providing expert analytical services, opportunities for exchange of experience with other developing-country authorities, technical and management advice, and long-term management reinforcement. Donors can also help identify opportunities for exposing parastatals to private competition or for divestment of profitable functions or sub-functions to private buyers. For example, donors helped the Government of Mali restructure its cereal board to allow private traders to compete for sales and distribution markets. The *Business and Industry*

Advisory Committee to the OECD (BIAC) has favoured these measures and argued that more official development assistance should be used to study possibilities for parastatal rehabilitation or privatisation. This could include evaluating enterprises or assets to be sold, and helping attract foreign investors.

Privatisation of state–owned enterprises is a major theme of the *United States* AID's dialogue with developing countries. AID views privatisation as a means of promoting competition and increasing employment, incomes, and living standards. In Costa Rica, AID helped the government establish a financial conduit to facilitate the phased divestiture or liquidation of enterprises held by the state holding company, CODESA. Parastatals accounted for 30 per cent of the public sector deficit in the past, but now 38 of the 42 CODESA corporations and affiliates are on track to be divested. Nine companies are in the process of sale, 20 are in the process of liquidation, seven have been transferred to other government agencies, and two will remain with CODESA. Companies that have been privatised were engaged in tuna processing, coffee subproducts, airlines, transportation, aluminium products, cotton ginning, and other agro–industrial enterprises.

Jamaica has used AID support to carry out significant privatisations, the most visible being the divestiture of the National Commercial Bank (NCB) in December 1986. This was designed to mobilise broad public support through the public sale of over 30 million shares of NCB stock. Apart from the nearly 2 000 NCB employees who invested, 15 000 applications were for under 300 shares, and 7 000 applications were for 300 to 1 000 shares. Over 70 per cent of Jamaica's Caribbean Cement Company was purchased through a share offer: 91 million shares were sold to 24 000 buyers, including 99 per cent of the company's employees. An additional 34 Jamaican enterprises are in various stages of privatisation, ranging from valuation to actual sale offerings.

The Centre for Privatisation, a private consortium supported by US AID, provides technical expertise for country and sector–specific privatisation strategies. The centre develops policy dialogue with host country public and private sector leaders, and helps to implement privatisation actions in selected countries. The Centre has provided technical assistance to over 40 countries. It has helped governments develop national privatisation plans in Honduras, the Philippines, and Thailand. It also provided advisers to the Government of Tunisia to analyse specific issues, and assisted the Government of Jordan to privatise the state–owned airline and the Amman city bus system.

France has a programme to provide bridging finance, training and advisory services to governments requesting assistance in their rationalisation and/or privatisation of parastatals.

Canadian parastatals provide technical assistance and management training to their counterparts in developing countries in fields such as energy, communications and transportation.

The *United Kingdom* provides assistance to parastatals in developing countries under normal bilateral aid arrangements.

Switzerland has financed for many years an UNCTAD technical assistance project concerning the purchase of agricultural products in developing countries. This assistance has often taken place in the framework of restructuring or even privatising the important enterprises concerned.

The *World Bank* has devoted substantial resources to improving public enterprises, and is trying to increase private sector involvement in areas traditionally reserved for the state. The Bank's infrastructure loans now stress management contracts, contracting out, and other forms of privatisation, and industrial projects are likely to emphasize restructuring (including privatisation and liquidation) over new investments. The Bank's decrease in lending to industrial public enterprises (from 7 per cent of total lending in 1981 to 0.7 per cent in 1987) reflects this shift. Privatisation activities include: changing public sector activities to reduce crowding out and increase the scope for private participation; privatising or liquidating state enterprises; contracting out government functions; replacing public monopolies with competing private businesses.

Bank projects helped Niger and Togo liberalise foodcrop marketing, Haiti did the same for flour imports, and Madagascar opened the rice trade to allow producers to sell to non–government traders. A structural adjustment loan (SAL) will help Togo lease its oil refinery tanks to the private sector; Jamaica will sign a management contract to run a sugar factory; and Morocco will allow the private sector to participate in fertilizer import and distribution. All of these measures were facilitated with assistance and support from the World Bank.

Since 1982, policy measures relating to public enterprises have constituted an important part of the work of the *International Monetary Fund* (IMF). The IMF has been active in public enterprise reform in 16 developing countries (Bolivia, Brazil, Burundi, Central African Republic, Côte d'Ivoire, Gabon, Guinea, Madagascar, Mali, Mauritania, Mexico, Morocco, Niger, Philippines, Togo and Uganda). In some cases (Brazil, Mexico) short–term measures (price adjustment, reduced investment, freezing of staff numbers) were needed to reduce financial burdens. In other instances, more fundamental restructuring was required (liquidation or privatisation, change in regulations, improving management and accounting). These long–term reform programmes were often undertaken in close collaboration with the World Bank. Analysing public enterprises' impact on a country's economy and identifying emerging problems and possible solutions have been an important part of this collaboration. The IMF and World Bank offer technical assistance in public enterprise reform. The required policies are monitored by the IMF through programme reviews and, as far as countries drawing on the structural adjustment facility are concerned, are included as "benchmarks" in financial arrangements with the Fund.

The *Asian Development Bank* (AsDB) has funded a number of privatisation studies and assisted in studies involving leasing arrangements, capital markets and venture capital financing. Most of AsDB's assistance to the private sector continues to be channelled through credit to development finance institutions.

6. ENCOURAGEMENT OF FOREIGN DIRECT INVESTMENT (FDI)

Foreign direct investment (FDI) has won more appreciation by developing countries as the costs of excessive borrowing for state enterprises have been recognised. Economic growth has been found to depend largely on private enterprise and investment. The debt crisis has curtailed private lending to developing countries, and official development assistance has not substantially taken up the slack. Under these circumstances, most developing countries have stepped up their efforts to attract foreign investment, not only for its contributions to their productive capital but also for its technology, training, management, and international marketing advantages.

DAC Members engage a number of means to encourage investors to look to developing–country markets: bilateral investment treaties; investment guarantee schemes; liberal outward investment rules; double taxation agreements; information and promotion services; development finance companies; incentives for joint ventures. Multilateral agencies also encourage FDI to developing countries through dispute settlement mechanisms, investment guarantees, promotion and protection agreements, and innovative investment schemes. See chapter III for details.

a) Bilateral and Multilateral Investment Treaties and Arrangements for the Settlement of Investment Disputes

Numerous *bilateral investment treaties* have been concluded by industrialised countries with a number of developing countries. These treaties contribute to a better investment climate in the host country and encourage private economic co–operation by establishing international investment norms [see "Intergovernmental Agreements Relating to Investment in Developing Countries", OECD, 1985]. *Germany* has signed 60 bilateral investment treaties — more than any other DAC Member. The agreements generally provide for unrestricted transfer of capital and earnings, fair and equitable treatment, and objective mechanisms for resolution of investors' disputes with host governments.

The *International Centre for Settlement of Investment Disputes (ICSID)* of the World Bank Group is an autonomous international institution which came into operation in 1966. By 1989 the number of contracting states (which have to be members of the World Bank and party to the Statute of the International Court of Justice) had increased to 97. Since its inception ICSID has handled some 23 investment disputes. ICSID promotes foreign investment through its publications, *Investment Laws of the World*, *Investment Treaties Series*, and the ICSID Review, *Foreign Investment Law Journal*.

b) Investment Guarantee Schemes

All *DAC Members* except Norway (which has suspended the old guarantee system pending the adoption of a new one) have investment guarantee schemes covering non–commercial risks. They insure against losses due to blockage of transfer in convertible currencies of capital or dividends to the insured foreign investor, straight and "creeping" expropriation, and war or civil strife. At the end of 1986, $20 billion (or 11 per cent of the $182 billion total investment stock in developing countries held by DAC country enterprises) were covered by investment guarantees. In absolute terms, Japan, with $10 billion, accounted for half this total, followed by the United States ($4 billion) and Germany DM 4.4 billion ($2 billion). Detailed descriptions of DAC Members' investment guarantee schemes are included in Chapter III.

A new member of the World Bank Group, the *Multilateral Investment Guarantee Agency* (MIGA), helps developing countries attract foreign investment by insuring investors against non–commercial risks, by providing member governments with advice on how to attract foreign investment, and by facilitating exchanges of experience on investment promotion and regulation among developing countries. MIGA was inaugurated in June 1988 by an initial group of 42 countries. Since then, membership has grown; by April 1989, 15 developed and 58 developing countries had signed the

MIGA Convention. MIGA guarantees against losses due to transfer restrictions, expropriation, breach of contract by host government, and war, revolution, or civil disturbance. Coverage is available for direct and portfolio equity, loans and loan guarantees, production or profit–sharing agreements, technical service and management contracts, franchising, licensing, leasing and turnkey contracts. Before issuing coverage, MIGA must be satisfied that a proposed investment is economically sound and contributes to the host country's development, and the host government must approve MIGA's guarantees and the risks to be covered. By complementing and supplementing existing coverage, MIGA expands the capacity and range of available investment insurance.

MIGA's Consultative and Advisory Services help member governments develop strategies to promote productive foreign investment. This includes consultative mechanisms under which developing country members can learn from each other effective means of attracting FDI. The jointly managed IFC–MIGA technical assistance facility, the Foreign Investment Advisory Service (FIAS), is being expanded to act for the World Bank Group in this field. MIGA should provide a forum for co–operation between investors and host countries, and a source of precedents for defining international law in respect of the rights of foreign investors and host governments. This role stems from the fact that it is financed and controlled jointly by developed and developing countries.

To promote a propitious investment climate, the *European Community* and African, Caribbean, Pacific (ACP) contracting parties conclude investment promotion and protection agreements. They may also conclude project–specific agreements in individual sectors. The European Commission is studying investment guarantee systems and the flow of FDI to ACP States as part of its Lomé III programme.

The IFC's Guaranteed Recovery of Investment Principal (GRIP) is an experimental means of expanding foreign direct investment in developing countries by relieving private investors of the risk of capital loss. In a GRIP deal the investor puts up the project capital and receives an IFC non–interest bearing note in return. IFC then makes the investment, assuming full responsibility for loss of principal. At the end of an agreed period the investor may extend the agreement, buy out IFC and become direct owner of the shares, or walk away from the deal with his principal intact. Like all IFC investments, GRIP must benefit the host country and show financial promise. GRIP deals are designed to attract non–traditional investors such as equipment suppliers and hotel chains, who rely on international business but cannot make sales without equity for their projects. GRIP is intended to meet the needs of all parties: the developing country benefits from equity capital inflows, the investor knows his equity is safe, and the IFC increases the flow of investment to the developing world without tying up its own money.

Another innovation to encourage private foreign investment is the *build, operate, transfer (BOT) scheme*. In a BOT deal a foreign syndicate of contractor(s), equipment supplier(s), and financial investor(s) finances and builds a large infrastructure project like a power plant, bridge or refinery, then runs the plant as a majority shareholder in a joint venture with the host government. After ten to fifteen years, the plant is sold, usually to the state. The contractor has a vested interest in the project's success since his return on capital will partly depend on how well the plant functions. The host government gains foreign management and capital, and international lenders win creditworthy customers. The US Eximbank and France's COFACE have both supported a BOT project in Turkey, along with Morgan Guaranty Bank, and three large contractors: Westinghouse, Kraftwerk Union and Chiyoda.

The World Bank has initiated a BOT scheme for energy development in Pakistan. The pilot programme entails major structural changes to put into place the institutional framework for the private sector. The Bank and bilateral and multilateral aid agencies have financed a private sector energy development fund which will provide long–term financing and up to 30 per cent of the total costs of BOTs. By July 1989 around $700 million had been mobilised.

c) Liberalisation of Outward Investment

Outward direct investment is unrestricted in the following DAC Member countries: *Belgium, Canada, Germany, the Netherlands, Switzerland, the United Kingdom* and *the United States*. Some countries require prior authorisation in all cases (*Norway*) or for investments exceeding a certain amount (*Denmark* for investments exceeding DKr 10 million and *Japan* for amounts of more than 10 million Yen). In some countries capital export authorisation depends on the investment's expected impact on the host country and on the home country's balance of payments (*Australia, Austria, Finland*, and *New Zealand*). *France* makes a distinction between capital export to countries of the franc area (which is free), to EEC member countries (which require prior notification), and to other countries (which require official authorisation if the amounts exceed FF 1 million per year and which have to be financed from foreign resources). In *Italy* no authorisation is required but the lira equivalent of 50 per cent of the foreign investment has to be deposited in a non–interest bearing account in the transferring bank. *Swedish* residents are authorised to transfer capital if the investment is financed with foreign capital — except for investments in sales companies, investments requiring less then SKr 1 million, and investments in developing countries receiving the bulk of Swedish aid. Details on DAC Members' policies concerning the treatment of outward direct investment are available in Chapter III.

d) Fiscal Measures

Most *DAC countries* have concluded bilateral agreements with developing countries to avoid double taxation. In the absence of a double taxation treaty most industrialised countries have special legal provisions to mitigate the effects of double taxation, such as tax deferral, tax credit systems and the fictitious tax credit. Detailed information on DAC Members' fiscal treatment of outward investment is presented in Chapter III.

e) Information and Promotion Services

Most *DAC countries* have information and promotion services on direct investment in developing countries, and many partially reimburse the costs of pre–investment and feasibility studies.

Investment promotion and export diversification are important components in many of the *United States* AID programmes. Twelve AID Missions in the Latin American and Caribbean region have help establish investment and export promotion organisations to attract US investors and assist local exporters. These organisations' services include: feasibility and marketing studies, joint venture brokering, legal and investor advice, and promotion of non–traditional exports. An example of such an organisation is the Coalition for Development Initiatives (CINDE) in Costa Rica, which has developed low–cost techniques for identifying potential foreign investors, helping them examine investment opportunities, and facilitating their establishment in Costa Rica. The two–year result has been the launching of 90 foreign projects in a country of 2.4 million people, involving investments totalling $118 million, which are expected to create over 16,000 jobs and export more than $100 million annually. Much of this success is attributable to Costa Rica's attractive political and economic environment, but here, too, CINDE has helped by successfully advocating changes in export incentives and financial legislation that make investing there more attractive.

In Egypt, an AID–supported investment promotion office has assisted over 100 companies. In Tunisia, AID helped the government rewrite its investment code in an effort to increase foreign direct investment.

In the framework of co–operation between members of the *European Communities* (EC) and states in Africa, the Caribbean and Pacific (ACP), the first Lomé Convention launched inter–enterprise co–operation by creating the Centre for the Development of Industry (CDI). The CDI partially finances feasibility or pre–investment studies and organises joint ventures between ACP and EC enterprises. By the end of 1984, it had contributed to the creation or recovery of 41 enterprises, generated nearly 3,000 jobs, and facilitated investment of about 77 million ECU. CDI has also provided some 150 developing country enterprises with expertise and training.

In addition to financing projects, the *European Commission* has launched a number of industrial promotion activities. These activities range from funding pre-feasibility studies for regional export industries to publishing manuals on how to set up firms in the ACP countries. Information on ACP country investment codes and industrial promotion programmes for certain countries (Senegal, Mauritius) is also available. The European Development Fund finances meetings between European and ACP promoters to facilitate inter–enterprise co–operation: following the West African Industrial Forum (whose sixth meeting brought over 300 European industrialists to Dakar in 1984) a similar programme was held in Libreville in December 1985 for the Central African countries.

The *United Nations Industrial Development Organisation* (UNIDO) has established seven investment promotion centres in cities in DAC Member countries (Cologne, New York, Paris, Tokyo, Vienna, Zurich and Milan). The UNIDO service is designed to strengthen ties between home country investors and developing countries, and to promote investment projects and technology transfer. It assists in identifying industrial investment opportunities in developing countries and draws investors' attention to project proposals. The services are offered free of charge to private and public institutions and financing agencies in developing and industrialised countries. UNIDO publishes industrial development reviews and organises investment symposia in developing countries. UNIDO also extends direct support to create or rehabilitate enterprises in developing countries.

f)   Public Development Finance Corporations

Ten DAC Members have established *Public Development Finance Corporations* (PDFCs) to encourage private investment in developing countries. PDFCs act as investment bank and development agency, and they can exert considerable leverage in mobilising foreign and local capital. They include the *Commonwealth Development Corporation* (CDC) in the United Kingdom, the *German Finance Company for Investments in Developing Countries* (DEG), the *Industrialisation Fund for Developing Countries* (IFU) in Denmark, the *Netherlands Finance Company for Developing Countries* (FMO), the *Belgian Corporation for International Investment* (SBI), the *Caisse centrale de coopération économique* (CCCE) in France, the *Swedfund* (Fund for Industrial Co-operation with Developing Countries) in Sweden, the *Finnfund* in Finland, the *Overseas Private Investment Corporation* (OPIC) in the United States, and a number of institutions in Japan. Chapter III describes each of these corporations.

PDFCs take minority positions in projects financed by home and/or host country investors. Most of them can invest in both debt and equity securities issued by enterprises in developing countries and do not normally require host country guarantees or collateral for their loans. All of these institutions, however, require host government approval of the projects they finance.

Participating investors from the industrialised countries usually trust PDFCs because of their rigorous financial standards and because they add a certain degree of political security to investments. Host country governments appreciate PDFCs because they insure "good developmental behaviour" by the foreign enterprise. PDFCs can also improve the standing of the enterprise with the banking community and the relationships between local and foreign investors. Once the enterprise is on stream and profitable, the PDFCs offer to sell their equity shares to their partners, with preference to recipient country residents. The proceeds of the equity sale are then reinvested in other ventures.

The PDFCs' basic criteria for projects and partners are soundness, profitability, and economic impact on home and host country economies. Preference is given to small and medium-sized enterprises in the partner countries. For example, OPIC's direct lending is available only to small American firms (defined as those that do not figure on the "Fortune 1000 list"). The *Business and Industry Advisory Committee* to the OECD has recommended that PDFCs not limit their activities to small companies within their own countries, but enlarge their scope to include large enterprises and enterprises from other countries.

PDFCs maintain frequent contact with their bilateral counterparts and with international organisations such as the World Bank, IFC, the Asian, African and Caribbean Development banks and the IDB. PDFCs in EEC Member countries have set up an informal association called Interact to promote co-operation among the association's members.

Like the bilateral PDFCs, the *International Finance Corporation* (IFC) invests in equity and makes loans, but it also underwrites securities offerings, provides standby financing, and organises commercial banks' participation in its loans. As of 30th June 1987, IFC's portfolio contained loans and equity investments in 404 companies in 77 countries with a total disbursement of $1.9 billion. IFC is increasingly concentrating its investments on rehabilitating existing companies. This is in line with structural adjustment programmes that emphasize re–organisation, privatisation, and lending to small and medium–sized enterprises.

g) Incentives for Joint Ventures

The *European Investment Bank* (EIB) provides risk capital for a variety of purposes, in particular to finance the acquisition of capital holdings. Lomé III earmarks an additional 600 million ECU for these operations.

Italy has launched a $100 million soft loan fund to promote joint ventures in developing countries. Financial assistance will be provided through concessional loans to Italian enterprises wishing to establish joint ventures in developing countries. Preference will be given to projects in agriculture and industry in countries receiving substantial amounts of Italian aid.

Canada provides various incentives to Canadian firms interested in establishing joint ventures in developing countries.

In *Denmark*, the Industrialisation Fund for Developing Countries (IFU) co-operates with Danish and local partners in direct investment in developing countries. With a capital fund of $155 million in 1988, IFU had participated in 140 projects in 50 countries. IFU contracted investments totalling $54 million in 13 new projects in 1988, and has also published a guide of Danish enterprises interested in setting up joint ventures with developing country partners.

In *France*, the Company for Promotion and Participation in Development (PROPARCO), a CCCE affiliate, promotes small and medium–sized joint ventures between French technical experts and national investors of developing countries. The PROPARCO participates through temporary minority shareholdings and helps to administer investment projects. The Centre of Industrial Promotion in Africa (CEPIA) and the Company for Industrial Promotion and Management (SOPROGI) promote African business ventures.

Japan created the ASEAN/Japan Development Fund in December 1987. ASEAN members agreed to take steps to boost inter–regional trade and stimulate the creation of joint ventures. It was also decided to relax existing bureaucratic rules to allow foreign investors in ASEAN Member States to take up to 60 per cent of the equity instead of the 49 per cent ceiling normally set by some ASEAN countries.

In 1976, the *New Zealand* Government set up the Pacific Islands Industrial Development Scheme, which offers incentives to New Zealand entrepreneurs for manufacturing and agro–businesses in the South Pacific Forum. The financial incentives include interest–free loans of up to 30 per cent of capital expenditure, and grants of up to 50 per cent of the cost of feasibility studies or the training of island staff. Island country businesses enjoy preferential access to many export markets (duty–free access for most goods to Australia and New Zealand and favoured access to EC countries under the Lomé Convention). The island countries have tried to improve their investment prospects through various incentives including tax and duty concessions, soft loans from development banks, and import protection.

The *United Nations Industrial Development Organisation* (UNIDO) organises joint venture promotion programmes and publishes a *Manual on the Establishment of Industrial Joint Venture Agreements in Developing Countries*. UNIDO also promotes enterprise–to–enterprise co–operation through its training, information, and research and advisory services.

7. ACTION BY NON–GOVERNMENTAL ORGANISATIONS (NGOs)

Non–governmental organisations (NGOs) can deliver benefits to the poor directly and at low administrative cost. Some NGOs stimulate private initiative by helping poor people mobilise and manage their own resources. Through training, technical advice, and credit, NGOs are strengthening the capacity of small farmers, tradesmen, and craftsmen to help themselves. A number of NGOs are catalysing institutional changes that make it possible for poor people to get credit, training, and other business assistance.

a) Official Support for Non–Governmental Organisations (NGOs)

All DAC Members give financial support to NGOs. A number of UN agencies and the World Bank and regional development banks also co–operate with NGOs. Several DAC Members have taken measures to encourage, organise and subsidise private groups which help transfer technical and managerial skills to private enterprises in developing countries. Business councils have been set up to provide consultant services to find practical solutions for in–plant problems. Several DAC countries have established senior executive services to provide management assistance and advice on productivity and new investment. Examples in the *United States* are the International Executive Service Corps and the Volunteers in International Technical Assistance; in *France* the association of retired experts, Echanges et consultations techniques internationaux; in *Germany* the Senior Expert Service; in *Japan* the International Management Association of Japan; in *Canada* the Canadian Executive Service Overseas; in the *United Kingdom* the British Executive Services Overseas; and in the *Netherlands* the Management Consultancy Programmes. The concept of reimbursable technical assistance may reflect an appropriate form of development co–operation when there are opportunities to generate additional revenue to cover technical assistance costs.

The *German* Government supports foundations which engage in small and medium–size enterprise development (mainly through advice and credit) and which, with employers associations and trade unions, strengthen recipient countries' negotiating capacities, labour market institutions, and research efforts. Germany's Federal Ministry for Economic Cooperation (BMZ) has conducted research which concluded that developing–country NGOs had an important role to play in helping local groups organise themselves. The BMZ research also highlighted the creditworthiness of the poor, which is illustrated by the reimbursement rate of borrowers to the Grameen Bank in Bangladesh.

The *Netherlands* has initiated co–operation between its aid agency and employers and trade union institutions to study the relationship between recipient country labour markets and the development assistance programme.

The *United States* supports small–scale and micro–enterprise development activities through institutional intermediaries, including private and voluntary organisations, co–operatives, national development foundations, credit unions, small business associations, and intermediate financial institutions. AID grants to the Institute for International Development led to loans for over 1,600 small enterprises, for example. In Bangladesh, AID supports an advisory service which funds small businesses there.

43

AID's Bureau for Food for Peace and Voluntary Assistance supports micro–enterprises in Africa, Asia, and Latin America.

b) NGO Activities

A number of European NGOs are extending credit guarantees to local borrowers through hard currency bank deposits.   The RAFAD foundation in *Switzerland* (Recherches et applications de financements alternatifs au développement) extends credit guarantees to groups or associations through the banking system and provides credit to partners rather than projects.

Women's World Banking (WWB), an independent non–profit organisation incorporated in the *Netherlands* and located in New York, promotes women entrepreneurship, particularly women who would not otherwise have access to credit.   It extends loan guarantees to banks and provides women entrepreneurs with technical and management advice.   Beneficiaries must be supported by a local affiliate group, usually a women's organisation, working with WWB.   WWB affiliates are active in some 50 countries.

France's Company for International Investment and Development (SIDI), which was initiated by the Catholic Committee Against Hunger and for Development, creates links between the informal and formal sector by investing and lending to small entrepreneurs.   The objective is to enable small–scale businessmen to gain access to their country's financial, commercial, and economic systems.   SIDI has traditionally operated by acquiring minority holdings in economically sound projects, but since 1986 SIDI has been setting up local investment companies.   Two companies have been established in Chile and Morocco, and two more are being set up in Thailand and Senegal.   Each company has as its shareholders one or more banks, SIDI and one or more similar companies, and local firms, organisations, and associations.   These investment companies provide persons or groups who would otherwise not have access to normal finance with the means to engage in business.   SIDI's finance and assistance have helped grassroots organisations work within the banking system.

Churches in some DAC countries provide credit to micro–enterprises in developing countries that have no access to commercial credit.   In *Sweden*, the Government supports long–term activities of NGOs, e.g., volunteer and church organisations which assist small and medium–sized industries.

The *German Chambers of Arts and Crafts* have extended their activities to developing countries.   Several partnerships between a German Chamber of Arts and Crafts and self–help organisations in the Third World are operating or under negotiation, either as a private venture or as part of a government agreement.   The programme is designed to promote self–help groups and small–scale enterprises.

The German Kolping Werk has long experience in helping small–scale enterprises with credits, advice, and in–house training.   The Kolping Werk shares this experience by extending its services to small entrepreneurs of developing countries.

III

MEASURES TAKEN BY INDIVIDUAL DONORS AND OTHERS TO PROMOTE FOREIGN DIRECT INVESTMENT IN DEVELOPING COUNTRIES

1. SUMMARY

Most DAC Members have policies and programmes to stimulate foreign direct investment in developing countries. Official aid has gone predominantly to support public sector investments, but private investors have made direct contributions in the productive sectors. Both official and private resource flows are important in the development process.

Some OECD countries retain administrative systems for the control of capital outflows, although in many cases requests for bona fide direct investment are granted automatically. In general, direct investments in developing countries are subject to very few restrictions.

The existing incentive programmes, which vary from one DAC country to another, can be grouped into the following categories:

a) Investment guarantee schemes covering political or non–commercial risks — i.e., risks which are outside the investor's control;

b) Fiscal treatment of investment income from developing countries;

c) Information and promotion activities, particularly the financing of pre-investment and feasibility studies;

d) Co–operation between government aid agencies and private foreign investors;

e) Government–sponsored investment corporations.

The possibilities for the capital–exporting countries to stimulate the flow of private capital to developing countries are rather limited. The major responsibility for the improvement of the investment climate remains with the host countries. In the past many developing countries introduced general or selective measures for the attraction, protection and promotion of foreign investment, and have frequently refined them.

Private investors find certain types of incentives provided by capital–exporting countries useful. Investors take advantage of fiscal incentives, guarantee programmes, publicly–financed feasibility studies or partnerships with public investment corporations. It is not possible, however, to determine the quantitative impact of these measures on the volume of foreign direct investment in developing countries.

Increasing use of the various incentive programmes in recent years has resulted from improvements made possible through experience. The governments of DAC Member countries exchange their experience in these fields at the OECD. These exchanges have been particularly helpful for countries establishing new programmes or revising existing ones.

2. INCENTIVE PROGRAMMES

A general summary of the various incentive programmes is provided below.

a) Investment Guarantee Schemes

All DAC Member countries have investment guarantee systems covering non–commercial risks. The schemes are sometimes restricted to certain categories of investment, mostly related to export operations. Experience has shown favourable reactions from investors, in particular for the coverage of small and medium–sized investments. Investment guarantees are not always limited to investments in developing countries. Guarantees are available only for new investments, i.e., for new projects or for expansion programmes.

Types of risk insured

Under most programmes, the non–commercial or political risks covered by the schemes are grouped into three categories.
— Expropriation risks: these include expropriation or nationalisation and confiscation without adequate compensation. In a number of schemes, the expropriatory action must have continued for at least one year before it is considered. While all schemes cover straight expropriation, the situation varies as regards "creeping expropriation", where the local enterprise is not taken over but its operation is impeded by government action to a point where it can no longer operate effectively.
— War risks, including revolution, rebellion and civil war. In order to retain an element of risk equivalent to that in developed countries, destruction resulting from a general war is in principle not covered.
— Transfer risks, essentially exchange control action taken after the conclusion of the guarantee contract and preventing or delaying the repatriation of profits and capital. This category excludes the risk of devaluation of the local currency. Also, in most programmes, local government action (other than exchange controls) which impedes actual repatriation falls under expropriation risks.

Types of investment guaranteed

Each scheme can provide coverage for different categories of capital participation in projects, such as: equity, inter–company lending, licences, royalties, etc.

46

Eligibility criteria

It is difficult to summarise the qualitative criteria which the various schemes demand of applications for guarantees. Most guarantee programmes specifically require that the investments further the economic development of the host country or that the project under consideration form part of its development programme. While the assessment of the developmental impact of investments may differ from one DAC country to another, guarantee schemes generally require that the projects be approved by the host government.

At the same time, many capital-exporting countries require that the projects provide economic advantages to their own economies. In particular, certain countries specifically cite the promotion of exports as an eligibility criterion.

In general, investment insurance portfolios are not concentrated on large companies. In fact, foreign investments of many large multinational companies often are not guaranteed against political risks.

Fees charged

Under some schemes, the three categories of risk can be covered separately, while other schemes charge a single fee for the three risks combined. Fees are normally standard fees, although a number of schemes make provision for lower or higher charges for particular situations or risks. Some countries offer premium rates for investors in joint ventures with local partners.

Provision is generally made for writing down over time the value of the investment guaranteed. Some countries look to the financial statements as in periodically audited accounts, while others adopt fixed schedules for writing down their value. Of the value thus established, under most schemes the investor himself bears a fraction of the risk in case of a loss; and indemnities paid usually represent around 90 per cent of the loss.

The coverage of earnings can be defined either under a global ceiling (e.g. a percentage of the original investment) or under an annual limit (e.g. 8 per cent per annum for up to three years).

The maximum duration of coverage is usually between fifteen and twenty years.

Prerequisite of investment protection agreements

Most DAC countries have concluded investment protection agreements with developing countries. Investment guarantees in these cases are provided, as a rule, only for investments in countries having signed such agreements. One of the main purposes of these agreements is to secure protection against discriminatory legal and administrative action, both as compared to the local business community and as compared to investors from other countries. The agreements do not always provide full and automatic protection against nationalisation. But the host country undertakes at least to provide fair compensation without undue delay. Agreements can be either detailed agreements of substance dealing with a number of issues such as guarantees, financial transfers, entry permission for foreign personnel, etc., or agreements limited to more procedural matters in the event that investments should be endangered.

Since these agreements appear to have provided effective protection for investments, as well as encouragement to foreign investors, new agreements continue to be negotiated and signed.

Guarantees for multinational projects

Large and medium–sized projects are increasingly being undertaken jointly by investors of more than one DAC country. With the present patchwork of national guarantee schemes, some investment partners can obtain investment guarantees but others cannot. Not only is there the problem of industrialised countries which have no scheme, but the definition of the "nationality" of the investing corporations used by the schemes is sometimes lacking in compatibility. The finance ministers of the EEC Member countries have therefore agreed on a directive to permit transnational co–insurance in the EEC, which came into force in 1980.

b) **Fiscal Measures**

There are several DAC countries which, upon acknowledging that taxes are paid abroad, exempt foreign income or offer a credit against foreign tax levied on world income. In other countries, foreign taxes may only be deducted as expenses, thereby leaving foreign investment at a disadvantage (tax exemptions granted by a developing country may be nullified with the result of higher tax liabilities in the capital–exporting country). Special tax incentives for domestic investment can work as a disincentive to foreign investment. Thus, in the absence of adequate tax treaties, foreign investment in developing countries may be less attractive than investment at home or in other industrialised countries. Until recent years, developing countries themselves appear to have been reluctant to conclude treaties because the present pattern of tax conventions relies mainly on taxation in the country of residence and tends to favour capital–exporting countries.

At present, conventions signed between developed and developing countries follow the structure and a number of substantive provisions of the OECD Model Double Taxation Convention. However, as was envisaged by the OECD Committee on Fiscal Affairs, the majority of such conventions allocate greater taxing rights to the developing country for dividends, interest, royalties and technical services than the OECD Model. The definition of what constitutes a permanent establishment is also generally wider than in the OECD Model. In addition, a number of these conventions contain tax sparing or other special provisions.

c) **Investment Information and Promotion Activities**

Investment opportunities in developing countries can only be realised if potential investors are adequately informed. More active information programmes by capital–exporting and, even more, by capital–importing countries are necessary to make businessmen familiar with economic conditions and opportunites in developing countries.

The basic services in this field offered by the governments of industrialised countries are provided by the traditional economic and commercial information centres found in national administrations, and in specialised agencies at home and diplomatic missions abroad. Most DAC countries have developed information systems for the dissemination of investment possibilities to national investors. Moreover, many DAC governments provide funds for the financing of pre–investment surveys and feasibility studies. Governments finance part — usually 50 per cent — of the cost of the survey, and the potential investor may have to reimburse its share of the cost if the project materialises.

d) Co-operation between Government Aid Agencies and Private Investors

Most DAC governments co-operate with private firms in developing countries by offering financial aid and technical assistance. Special programmes or funds for government loans to firms from DAC countries wishing to invest in developing countries have been set up, e.g., in Austria, France, Germany, Japan and the United States. In addition, loans are sometimes extended to private firms operating in developing countries out of the ordinary aid programmes. Moreover, most countries have official export credit programmes to finance equipment exports. In some cases export credits have been decisive factors in the financing of private foreign investment.

e) Government-sponsored Investment Corporations

Ten OECD countries, all Members of the DAC, and the World Bank have established special public development finance corporations. These institutions invest directly in projects, usually in partnership with local and foreign investors. Most of them can invest in both loans and equity and do not ask for guarantees from the local government nor even, normally, collateral for their loans. All of these institutions, however, require host government approval of the projects they finance.

These corporations associate their limited public resources with a much larger volume of private funds. They perform a multiple role in promoting projects which are both commercially viable and have a developmental priority. They provide capital and related financial services, as well as technical assistance. But perhaps more important is their catalytic role. Far more involved than ordinary banking institutions in the evaluation of projects and financial arrangements, the corporations have frequently been responsible for bringing in other national and international investment partners. They are designed to mobilise private capital from their own countries, but can also associate with investors from other developed countries. The International Finance Corporation (IFC) finances projects jointly with investors from any Member country of the World Bank. The Inter-American Investment Corporation does the same with Members of the Inter-American Development Bank.

Investors from the developed world appreciate these public investment corporations because of their rigorous standards of financial appraisal and because they also bring a certain degree of security to investments in view of their official status. Local governments see such institutions as an assurance of "good developmental behaviour" by the foreign enterprises. Their participation also improves the standing of the enterprise with the banking community and the relationships between local and foreign investors.

The public corporations strike a careful balance between their dual objectives as both investment banks and development institutions. On the one hand, they are expected to operate on commercial lines and pay their own way, making profitable investments and thus offering an attractive basis for the association of outside resources. On the other hand, they are instruments of official development policy and are therefore concerned with developmental considerations. This implies that they normally restrict their intervention to priority sectors and projects, and abstain from a number of profitable projects which are not of clear developmental priority or which do not require long-term financial assistance. Their activity has been concentrated in manufacturing, energy, public utilities, agriculture, agro-business (particulary fertilizers), housing and tourism. While the ventures they assist are expected to operate commercially and to maximise profits, the institutions themselves are not expected to maximise their own profits and thus can provide financial services, and technical and financial assistance on relatively soft terms. The cost of these services is not generally imputed to the projects financed.

3. COUNTRY PROGRAMMES

A. Australia

Exchange Control

Investment overseas may be freely undertaken by Australian residents without restriction. The vast bulk of exchange control restrictions and requirements, including those relating to all forms of investment overseas, were abolished when the decision was made to float the Australian dollar in December 1983. There are, however, certain procedural requirements that may need to be met for taxation screening purposes before funds associated with such investments can be remitted from Australia.

Bilateral Investment Protection Agreements

So far, Australia has not signed any specific agreements with developing countries for the protection of foreign direct investment.

Investment Guarantee Scheme

The Overseas Investment Insurance Scheme, which was established in 1966, is administered on the Government's behalf by the Export Finance and Insurance Corporation (EFIC)[1]. It provides investment insurance against the three main categories of non–commercial risk, separately or combined. In 1974, in conformity with its announced policy of encouraging Australian direct investment abroad (made with local participation, with the approval of the host country and in Australia's national interest), the government liberalised the criteria applying to investment eligible for insurance. In 1976 the legislation was amended to expedite processing of the more routine applications by permitting EFIC to insure these on its own account, without reference to the Government for individual approval.

In 1986 EFIC and a number of export–supporting official organisations became part of the Australian Trade Commission (AUSTRADE).

The investments eligible for coverage may consist of equity participation or loans, and the form of transfer may be cash, machinery, equipment, and technical or managerial services. The insurance may cover up to 200 per cent of the value of the original investment (the "maximum amount" of insurance) to allow for insurance of accumulated earnings. The difference between the "maximum amount" and the "current amount" (which is the coverage provided on the basis of the current value of the investment of time), known as the "stand–by amount", provides a reserve which the investor may use to insure the increases in his participation in the foreign enterprise.

Remitted earnings are insured to a value of 20 per cent of net investment per year, up to 100 per cent in the first five years. Higher levels of cover may be allowed. The investor must attempt to transfer investment earnings within nine months of receipt. The liability in the event of loss will normally be not more than 90 per cent of the insured amount, the investor bearing the remaining 10 per cent. The coverage is normally extended for a minimum of five years and a maximum of 20 years. The premium for the three risks combined is 0.8 per cent for "current cover" plus 0.4 per cent for "stand–by cover". Each of the three risks can be insured separately at a premium of 0.32 per cent for expropriation and 0.24 per cent for exchange transfer blockage and war damage for "current cover", and half these rates for "stand–by".

The maximum contingent liability of EFIC on its own and the Government's behalf is $A750 million.

The total value of outstanding political insurance policies at the end of June 1987 was $A133 million (US$95 million), of which 60 per cent was in South–East Asian countries (members of ASEAN).

Fiscal Measures

Generally, Australian law makes no distinction between income from industrialised and developing countries. From 1st July 1987, the then–existing double taxation relief arrangements of the income tax law were replaced with a general foreign tax credit system (FTCS). Under the new system, all foreign income received by Australian residents (aside from certain wages and salary income, which may be partially or fully exempted) is subject to Australian tax, although a credit up to the amount of Australian tax payable is allowed for any foreign tax paid.

In order to avoid nullifying genuine development incentives offered by developing countries, Australia intends to provide tax sparing, on a country–by–country basis, either by regulations made for that purpose or by special provisions in comprehensive double taxation agreements. A limited amount of tax sparing is already provided for in agreements with a few developing countries.

Where tax sparing is granted, the tax forgone by the foreign country under particular tax incentive measures will be deemed to have been paid by the Australian taxpayer receiving income which benefits from the tax incentives, and will be allowed as a credit against Australian tax on the foreign income concerned.

Other Official Support

In 1981 the Australian International Development Assistance Bureau (AIDAB) introduced a joint venture scheme into its South Pacific Aid Programme. The aim of the scheme is to facilitate the creation of employment and generation of income in South Pacific countries through the establishment or expansion of businesses. It does this by using aid funds to assist South Pacific countries purchase equity in joint business ventures with Australian businesses. These funds are channelled through individual island governments in support of specific joint venture proposals. Although funds are not used to support the Australian partner in joint ventures, the effect of the scheme is to encourage investment by Australian partners. The scheme is currently under review with the objective of making it more responsive to the needs of recipients.

The Australian Trade Commission's Trade Commissioner service provides potential investors with detailed information on regulations, incentives and opportunities available in other countries.

The Department of Foreign Affairs and Trade, through its Market Advisory Service, assists the governments of some developing countries to promote investment opportunities in their countries in Australia. Funding and/or organisational assistance is provided for missions, seminars and production of promotional material. Programmed assistance is provided to ASEAN countries under the ASEAN Trade and Investment Promotion Programme (TIPP). Assistance to other developing countries is provided on a case–by–case basis.

B. Austria

Exchange Control

The transfer of capital for direct investment abroad is subject to the approval of the Austrian National Bank. The authorisation will be granted provided the investment will result in the establishment and maintenance of commercial relations with the Austrian investor.

Investment Protection Agreements

So far, Austria has not signed any specific agreements for the protection of foreign direct investment with developing countries.

Investment Guarantee Scheme

The Austrian investment guarantee scheme, which is administered by the Österreichische Kontrollbank (OKB)[2], applies to both industrialised and developing countries. It normally covers 90 to 100 per cent of the initial new investment in the form of equity participation, loans and licences. The investor may obtain an extension of the guarantee to include reinvested earnings. The premium for the coverage of the three main political risks combined is 0.5 per cent annually. The maximum duration of the cover is twenty–five years.

Fiscal Measures

Austria has signed a number of agreements on the avoidance of double taxation which are based on the principle of taxation at the source (i.e., profits earned and taxed in other countries are not taxable in Austria). Agreements of this kind are in force with Brazil, Egypt, Greece, India, Indonesia, Israel, Mexico, Pakistan, Portugal, Spain, and Turkey. In order to minimise double taxation of income earned in countries other than those mentioned above, an investor may apply to the financial authorities. A further facility is provided by the income tax law, which stipulates that investments made in Austria may be valued, for tax purposes, at 90 per cent of their costs. To benefit from this regulation, however, the participation of the Austrian investor has to exceed 25 per cent of the total capital of the foreign company.

Other Official Support

To promote the activities of Austrian enterprises in developing countries, the OKB initiated in 1964 a credit programme called "Start–up assistance" (Starthilfe Kreditaktion) with ERP (European Recovery Programme) funds and financial assistance from the Federal Economic Chamber. The credits are administered by a Committee composed of representatives from the Ministry of Foreign Affairs (Development Assistance Office), and the Ministries of Finance, Economic Affairs, Public Economy and Transport, as well as from the Federal Economic Chamber. The Committee evaluates each investment project with particular regard to its effect on the economy of the host country. Preferential treatment is given to joint ventures with local investors. The allocated amount which may be borrowed for projects in European developing countries for up to ten years (with a grace period of up to five years), and for projects in non–European developing countries for up to 20 years (with a grace period up to five years), should be covered by an investment guarantee. State subsidies enable the Kontrollbank to extend loans on relatively favourable terms at an interest rate of 5 to 6.5 per cent per annum. In 1974, the start–up credit scheme was reorganised and extended by the use of funds from the OKB's export financing scheme. From the end of 1977 onwards, start–up credits have been available in the form of refinancing credits to credit institutes.

The OKB also offers another form of financing of investment abroad which is not restricted to developing countries. Most of the conditions of these credits are similar to those of the "start–up" credits, but with higher interest rates. This instrument was added to enable the Kontrollbank to provide loans for projects requiring large amounts of finance. In fact, the two lending programmes may be combined to finance particularly large enterprises.

Finally, the Austrian development assistance programme provides funds for feasibility and pre–investment studies.

C. Belgium

Exchange Control

No authorisation is necessary to make a direct investment abroad, but the investor must submit a written declaration stating the purpose of the operation to a bank approved by the Belgium–Luxembourg Exchange Institute. On the basis of this declaration, the bank automatically effects the transfer via the free exchange market. For investments that serve to create or maintain sustained economic relations between the investor and the enterprise abroad, transfers via the official exchange market may be approved.

Bilateral Investment Protection Agreements

Belgium has signed investment protection agreements with Bangladesh, Cameroon, China, Egypt, Hungary, Indonesia, Malaysia, Morocco, Romania, Rwanda, Singapore, South Korea, Sri Lanka, Tunisia and Zaire.

Investment Guarantee Scheme

The scheme which guarantees Belgian direct investment abroad against political risk was established in 1971. Applicable throughout the world, the scheme is of particular importance for investment in developing countries. It is administered by the "Office National du Ducroire"[3], which is also the official export credit guarantee agency. The Board of Directors of the OND includes representatives of various ministries (Economic Affairs, Finance), including the General Directorate for Foreign Economic Relations and the General Administration for Development Co-operation (AGCD) of the Ministry for Foreign Affairs, Foreign Trade and Development Co-operation. To appraise the eligibility of an investment for a guarantee, the OND applies two broad criteria: *a)* the project must contribute to the economic and social development of the recipient country and *b)* it must promote Belgium's economic interests abroad.

In addition, the investment must be approved by the host country and must be protected either by the laws of that country or by a bilateral agreement between it and Belgium.

The guarantee covers the three main classes of political risk and occasionally the risk of unexpected natural disasters. The coverage applies both to the sum initially invested and to reinvested earnings up to a maximum of 50 per cent of the initial sum. It may also cover distributed profits up to 10 per cent per annum of the capital sum insured. The guarantee covers 90 per cent of the amount insured, to be reduced to 80, 70 and 60 per cent respectively during the last three years of insurance.

The maximum duration of the guarantee is fifteen years from the date of completion of the investment or twenty years from the date of issue of the policy. The premium for all risks combined is 0.75 per cent per annum of the current amount or 0.8 per cent if earnings are included. At the end of 1981, the OND had outstanding investment insurance policies for a total of US$34 million. In 1987 alone, policies issued by OND represented a total of US$20 million.

Tax Measures

In cases where there are no double taxation agreements, Belgian taxes on foreign earnings that have already been taxed abroad are reduced to one-quarter or one-half of the normal amount, depending on whether the beneficiary is a company or an individual. Where double taxation agreements exist, such income is taxed in the foreign country only. Belgium has signed double taxation agreements with India, Indonesia, Israel, Malaysia, Morocco, Pakistan, the Philippines, Singapore, South Korea, Thailand, Tunisia, Turkey and Zaire.

In practice, Belgium already unilaterally exempts from all tax the dividends from permanent holdings, irrespective of size, in foreign companies (e.g., dividends from foreign subsidiaries). Under ordinary law, Belgium reduces the tax on other foreign investment income by 15 per cent of the net income after foreign tax. In its tax conventions with developing countries, Belgium further applies the "tax sparing credit" or notional credit principle, thus offsetting against its own tax, within certain limits, the taxes temporarily forgone by the developing countries as a stimulus to investment.

The "Fonds de la Coopération au Développement" (FCD)

The Belgian Fund for Development Co-operation (FCD), established under an Act of 10th August 1981, became operational at the beginning of 1983. It is managed by the General Administration for Development Co-operation (AGCD)[4].

The FCD constitutes a new tool for financing productive investment in developing countries through participation in national or regional development banks or in public enterprises or joint ventures, mainly in the manufacturing sector[5]. Its financial resources come principally from the Belgian bilateral co-operation budget, and in 1988 were estimated to amount to BF 10 billion (US$250 million).

In creating the FCD, Belgium has complemented its institutions to promote Belgian investment abroad. The "Société Belge pour l'Investissment International" (SBI, see below) was, in fact, established for the purpose of financing foreign investment in both developing and developed countries to promote Belgian interests abroad, whereas the FCD is designed to promote economic and social development in developing countries. Thus, to be eligible for financing, projects must not only meet developmental considerations but also be economically viable. Host countries are expected to provide adequate protection of foreign direct investment and to guarantee that capital and earnings may be freely repatriated.

Target countries for FCD activities are mainly those with which Belgium has concluded co-operation agreements. At least 25 per cent of the Fund's resources must be allocated to projects in low-income countries. Financial support by the Fund may take the form of loans, interest subsidies or equity participation. Loans or credit lines are provided on terms which vary according to the nature of the projects and the stage of development of the recipient country, but carry a grant element of at least 25 per cent. Subsidies of up to 3 per cent may be granted on interest due on loans for productive investment; the Fund can also provide guarantees with respect to loans qualifying for an interest subsidy. It may also put up venture capital for feasibility studies for FCD-financed investment projects. If it is decided to go ahead with the project, the costs involved are incorporated as part of the Fund's participation. If it is decided not to go ahead, the costs are shared equally between the Fund and its partners.

Financial co-operation between the FCD and joint ventures is governed by the following rules:

— The public sector must have a majority stake in the joint venture (the "public sector" for this purpose may be an enterprise whose liabilities are underwritten by a central government or a national/regional development bank);
— The Fund's contribution must constitute not less than 10 per cent and no more than 30 per cent of the capital;
— Belgian private investment must at least match the Fund's contribution, except in the case of investment in the least developed countries;
— The Belgian partners must play a major role in the joint venture's management;
— The host country authorities must have approved the investment.

The "Société Belge d'Investissement International" (SBI)

The Belgian International Investment Corporation (SBI)[6] was set up jointly by the Belgian public and private sectors. Its shareholders are the "Société National d'Investissement", which has a majority equity stake, the "Banque Nationale de Belgique", the "Caisse Générale d'Epargne et de Retraite", and a number of private banks and industrial and service enterprises, including "La Générale de Banque", the "Banque Bruxelles Lambert" and "Tractebel".

The role of the SBI is to contribute to the medium– and long–term financing of foreign business ventures which help to promote economic relations between Belgium and the host countries. It can participate in a variety of ways such as business creation or the acquiring, merging, expanding or modernising of existing concerns.

The SBI may be involved in projects world–wide, including developing countries in Africa, Asia and Latin America. It has participated in many ventures throughout North America and Europe. It has a particular interest in investment in the EC countries.

SBI involvement is usually via minority holdings and/or loans and convertible or non–convertible medium– and long–term bonds. It varies according to requirements and may take the form of joint participation.

In its financial partnership role the SBI backs up the action of Belgian and/or foreign economic operators. It may also lend to Belgian enterprises part of the funds they need for their own investment abroad.

In addition to its standard range of activities outlined above, the SBI can offer other financial techniques such as leasing or lease–back, syndicated loans and under-writing.

The SBI has built up an extensive network of contacts and co–operates with a large number of Belgian and foreign companies as well as with international development institutions, especially the World Bank and the EEC. It draws on these contacts in choosing, preparing and cofinancing projects, and in finding partners.

With its experience and specialised knowledge, the SBI is also well placed to brief and advise the corporate sector on investing abroad.

The SBI is especially interested in promoting and supporting technically and economically sound projects that are both profitable and of value to the community. Here, the quality of the feasibility studies is crucial, along with that of project administration and management which, at least in the initial stages, will involve a contribution by enterprises with experience in the field.

Among the sectors, importance is given to agro–industry (21 per cent), followed by metal manufactures (19 per cent), with other sectors such as building materials and construction, services, chemicals and chemical engineering — each accounting for around 10 per cent.

At 30th September 1987, investment totalling BF 961 billion had been committed for 53 ventures.

Broken down by region, project commitments were as follows:

Europe	(31 per cent)
North America	(24 per cent)
Africa	(26 per cent)
Latin America	(15 per cent)
Asia	(4 per cent)
Industrialised Regions	(55 per cent)
Developing Regions	(45 per cent)

SBI activities in developing countries

The BF 490 million invested in the 28 ventures implemented or authorised at 30th September 1987 in developing countries account for around 48 per cent of the Corporation's total portfolio commitments or authorisations. The SBI estimates the actual or planned investment in these countries involving SBI financing at around BF 14.7 billion, 30 times its own contribution. This ratio, highly advantageous to the host countries, is due to the partnership and cofinancing arrangements in which the SBI has played a part.

	The SBI's operations in developing countries 1982/83–1986/87									
	Number					Amount (BF/million)				
	86/87	*85/86*	*84/85*	*83/84*	*82/83*	*86/87*	*85/86*	*84/85*	*83/84*	*82/81*
Authorised in LDCs	5	2	7	3	4	116	22	116	46	76
Total authorised	11	6	2	8	11	265	82	249	125	185
Committed in LDCs	2	4	6	3	3	43	109	65	48	68
Total committed	8	7	9	5	9	191	162	187	118	156

The SBI not only supplies developing countries with additional capital, it also makes available its considerable experience. It can provide information, research, consultancy services, contacts and introductions. What is more, successful projects may prove to be replicable and have a spreading effect.

Other official support

The General Administration for Development Co–operation (AGCD) regularly commissions feasibility studies by research institutions for the benefit of developing countries and in agreement with them. In some cases it commissions Belgian firms to set up pilot plants or manage vocational training centres. Technical assistance in the management of a number of enterprises is provided by Belgian centres or firms under contract to the AGCD (and in compliance with public works regulations).

D. Canada

Bilateral Foreign Investment Insurance Agreements

Canada has entered into bilateral agreements on investments insured by the Export Development Corporation (EDC)[7] in the following 41 countries: Antigua, Bahamas, Barbados, Belize, Bolivia, Cameroon, Chile, China, Costa Rica, Dominica, Fiji, Gambia, Ghana, Grenada, Guinea, Guyana, Haiti, Indonesia, Israel, Jamaica, Jordan, Liberia, Malawi, Malaysia, Malta, Montserrat, Morocco, Pakistan, Papua New Guinea, Philippines, Rwanda, St. Kitts Nevis, Saint Lucia, Saint Vincent,

Senegal, Singapore, Sri Lanka, Thailand, Trinidad & Tobago, Western Samoa, and Yugoslavia.

Basically the bilateral agreement outlines the EDC's rights in the event of payment of a claim as recognised and approved in writing by the government of the host country.

The bilateral agreement specifically states that suitable arrangements are in effect through which EDC, if the need arises, could be assigned an insured investor's rights existing in that country as protected by an EDC insurance policy. The host government must approve the investment or the investment must be permitted by the laws of the host country.

Investment Guarantee Scheme

EDC provides foreign investment insurance that protects Canadians investing abroad against three frequently encountered political risks: 1) blocked transfer of funds, 2) expropriation, and 3) war, revolution or insurrection.

The investor has the option of applying for a policy covering any or all of the three risks.

Any person, corporation, government agency or other legal entity which is carrying on business or other activities in Canada, and is planning a new investment in a foreign country is eligible to apply. The investment can be made directly into a foreign enterprise, or indirectly through a related company based in Canada, the host country, or a third country.

Insurance is only available for new investments, that is investments for which funds have not been irrevocably committed previously.

It is the responsibility of the investor to obtain a statement from the host government giving its approval of the proposed project or activity, and of the investor's investment in it. This statement, which is called the Host Government Approval, is an official document issued by, or under the authority of, the government of the host country.

It is the Canadian investor's direct or indirect interest in the investment that is insurable, not the total investment from all sources.

In circumstances where there is more than one Canadian investor as a participant, each investor's interest is considered separately for an individual insurance policy.

EDC covers almost any right that an investor might acquire in a foreign enterprise, including equity, loans, guarantees, management contracts, and royalty and licensing agreements. The investment may be in the form of cash, contribution in kind, or the issuance of a financial guarantee.

Cover for investments is normally limited to a maximum period of 15 years but longer terms will be considered where warranted. The minimum period of coverage for equity investments is not fixed, but it is presumed that most investments in this category will be of a lasting nature.

The maximum amount insurable at the time of issuance of a policy in respect of the three political risks is up to 300 per cent of the dollar amount of the original investment for equity securities, and up to 200 per cent of the dollar amount of the original investment for debt securities.

In the case of management and technical services agreements, insurance covers the payment receivable for services rendered to a maximum of the annual payment receivable multiplied by the term of the agreement.

Fiscal Measures

The Canadian Income Tax Act does not make a distinction between income from investments in developing countries and those made in other countries. Tax–sparing, however, is granted under the provisions of specified double taxation conventions with developing countries. The most important measures available to Canadian investors are as follows:

a) Taxes on income or profit paid in the source country generally are eligible for credit against Canadian income taxes payable, this credit being limited to the amounts of Canadian taxes otherwise payable on such income.

b) Canada has double taxation conventions in force with several developing countries. These conventions not only provide for specific mechanisms to avoid double taxation, normally by way of a credit, but also reduce, and put a ceiling on, the rate of withholding tax that may be imposed on dividends, interest and royalties paid by a resident of one country to a resident of the other. In addition, Canadian residents are generally granted a credit for certain taxes which have not been paid if they fall within those specified in the conventions, e.g., a tax holiday granted by the developing country.

c) Business earnings of a subsidiary of a Canadian company are not subject to Canadian tax on an accrual basis if the subsidiary is not resident in Canada. A resident corporation is taxable in Canada, and a credit is granted for foreign taxes.

d) Dividends received by a Canadian company from a foreign company are taxable in Canada with relief from double taxation provided by way of a credit for the foreign withholding tax. Where the Canadian company has at least 10 per cent interest in the foreign company, further relief is provided by way of a credit for the underlying foreign tax paid by the corporation. When a double taxation convention is in force, the dividends received by such a corporation are exempt from corporate tax in Canada.

Other Official Support

The Canadian International Development Agency's (CIDA) Industrial Co–operation Programme (INC) helps Canadian companies underwrite part of the risk associated with investment opportunities in developing countries. Through the INC programme, Canadian business is encouraged to promote industrialisation in these countries through mutually beneficial investment, transfer of technology and joint ventures.

INC was established in 1978 to stimulate participation by the Canadian private sector in the industrial development of developing countries. INC programmes can help Canadian firms establish long–term business collaboration in developing countries by partially financing the development of joint ventures.

INC programmes support a number of activities, from identifying opportunities to assistance during the early stages of project operation. INC also provides funding to applicants who have identified specific business partners and are willing to put capital into the venture. When positive potential has been demonstrated as a result of preliminary investigation, assistance is provided to carry out viability studies, the aim of which is to conclude joint venture negotiations.

Joint ventures may include co–production or production–sharing agreements, assembly operations, or licensing agreements.

As part of its project approval process CIDA consults other federal government departments, diplomatic missions and regional financial institutions. The services provided by the Industrial Co–operation Division (INC) complement other programmes provided to the business community by the Department of External Affairs, Regional Industrial Expansion, the Export Development Corporation and provincial governments, which also provide information about investment opportunities in developing countries.

E. Denmark

Bilateral Investment Protection Agreements

Denmark has concluded bilateral agreements for the protection of direct investments with Malawi, Indonesia, Romania, Sri Lanka and China.

Investment Guarantee Scheme

The Danish investment guarantee scheme, which was established in 1966, is administered by the Danish International Development Agency (DANIDA)[8] in the Ministry of Foreign Affairs. The scheme provides coverage for the three main political risks for new direct investment in developing countries. In principle, the scheme applies only to those investments which give the investor a certain degree of control over an enterprise. Portfolio investments are therefore excluded, although long–term loans of an investment–like character may be covered. Only investments which have a positive developmental effect on the host country's economy are eligible. Investment guarantees are available for private commercial and industrial enterprises with registered offices in Denmark. The investor bears 10 per cent of the risk, depending on the existence of an investment protection agreement with the host country. The guarantee covers both the initial investment and earnings up to 20 per cent per annum for up to three years. Only coverage of the three risks combined is available at a premium of 0.5 per cent per annum. At the end of 1986 policies issued represented total liabilities of DKr 176 million ($25 million).

The Public Investment Corporation, IFU

The Industrialisation Fund for Developing Countries[9] was established in 1967 as a non–profit autonomous institution, based on the same principles as the British CDC and German DEG. Operations started in 1968 with the purpose of promoting investments in developing countries in co–operation with private Danish industry and, whenever possible, local investors. Although it is not required that the Danish partner control the enterprise, he should at least have a substantial influence on the company's management if the IFU is to be a partner. Economically viable joint ventures which are approved by the host country are eligible for cofinancing in all non–European developing countries and Turkey.

The IFU not only provides equity and loan financing but also feasibility studies, the transfer of know–how, and other services. As a rule, IFU's participation is limited to 35 per cent of the share and loan capital and will not exceed the Danish partner's holdings, although exceptions to this rule may be made for investments in the least developed countries. The IFU does not seek managerial responsibilities in joint ventures.

As regards sectors of activity, IFU concentrates on manufacturing and agro-business and on tourism, industrialised housing, consulting, engineering, and transportation, including local shipping. In exceptional cases IFU also participates in trading companies. Its financial assistance is not tied to the purchase of Danish equipment. The IFU will withdraw from a project when the enterprise has reached economic viability, usually after six to eight years of operation. Its partners in the enterprise have a priority right to acquire IFU's share.

The resources of IFU are supplied by the government. Its total assets, including retained earnings, amounted to DKr 1 111 million ($160 million) at the end of 1986. So far, IFU has participated in 112 projects, representing cumulative commitments of DKr 866 million ($125 million).

F. Finland

Investment Protection Agreements

Bilateral agreements for the protection of private investments have been signed with the Arab Republic of Egypt, Sri Lanka and Malaysia.

Investment Guarantee Scheme

The Finnish investment guarantee scheme, which came into operation in February 1981 and is administered by the Export Guarantee Board (Vientitakuulaitos VTL)[10], can cover investments in all developing countries on the DAC list. It provides a guarantee against the three main categories of political risks: expropriation, serious disturbance in the economic conditions of the host country, and restrictions in capital and earnings repatriation. All companies and institutions domiciled in Finland are eligible for investment guarantees, provided they can successfully carry out the investment. Investments may be in the form of equity participation in a foreign enterprise, and loans or loan guarantees to such an enterprise. Other forms of investment e.g., licences, are also possible. Reinvested earnings may be covered to the extent that such earnings at the time of reinvestment are freely transferable to Finland. Coverage can also be extended to remitted earnings up to 8 per cent per annum. The maximum period of coverage is twenty years and the minimum period is three years.

The investor is required to demonstrate that his project will provide economic benefits to Finland and the host country. The investment must always be approved by the host government. Coverage will be provided for projects which represent new investments, expansions, modernisations, or improvements of existing investments. The policy always covers all three risk categories. The annual premium for capital investment is 0.5 per cent and for remitted earnings 0.7 per cent. The maximum percentage of cover is 90 per cent. VTL's liability ceiling for investment guarantees is Mk 400 million ($93 million).

Fiscal Measures

Finland applies the same taxes on net income from foreign and domestic operations; but dividends, interest and royalties — other than those paid from Finland and connected with a foreign branch company in Finland — are taxed at the source on a gross income basis. Unless a double taxation agreement applies, foreign national income taxes on foreign source income may be credited against Finnish state (national) income tax. Depreciation allowances are the same for domestic and foreign operations. Agreements for the avoidance of double taxation have been concluded with Brazil, India, Israel, the Republic of Korea, Morocco, the Philippines, Singapore, Tanzania, Zambia, the Arab Republic of Egypt, Indonesia, Malaysia, Sri Lanka and Thailand. As a general rule these treaties provide for a proportionally higher taxation in the country where an investment has been made than do tax agreements between Finland and developed countries. Under these double taxation treaties a Finnish company will normally be exempt from a domestic tax on dividends from a foreign subsidiary. Finnish companies are tax–exempt when the "exemption" method is applied for avoiding double taxation on income from a foreign branch. When the "tax credit" method is used (as a general method or in relation to certain items of income) Finland has agreed to a credit for taxes spared through incentives granted by the contracting country.

The Public Development Finance Corporation, FINNFUND

The Finnish Fund for Industrial Development Co–operation Ltd. FINNFUND[11], was established by the Finnish Government in 1979. The Fund is a joint stock company with a capital of Mk 122 million (some $30 million), of which the Government's share is 92 per cent. The rest of the shares are held by the Finnish Export Credit Ltd., the Industrialisation Fund of Finland Ltd., and the Confederation of Finnish Industries. The Fund is subordinated to the Ministry of Foreign Affairs. The following ministries and institutions are represented on its Board of Directors: the Department for International Development and Co–operation in the Ministry of Foreign Affairs (FINNIDA), the Ministry of Trade and Industry, the Ministry of Finance, the Department for Foreign Trade in the Ministry of Foreign Affairs, the Finnish Export Credit Ltd. and the Industrialisation Fund of Finland Ltd.

Investment of government funds through FINNFUND are made on terms qualified as official development assistance. The purpose of FINNFUND is to contribute to economic and social development in developing countries through participation in their industrialisation efforts. The Fund promotes the initiation, establishment and expansion of joint ventures between local and Finnish entrepreneurs. Although FINNFUND operations cover their own costs, the Fund's activities are in line with the Finnish development aid programme, e.g., using the OECD Development Assistance Committee's lists for the selection of beneficiary countries and taking into account the special needs of the least developed countries. Loans granted by FINNFUND are normally in Finnish marks or other convertible currencies. Loans of up to fifteen years maturity normally have a grace period of two to three years and an interest rate of 4 to 7 per cent. It is assumed that investment denominated in local currency is financed by borrowing on the local financial market and through local equity participation. At the end of 1987 FINNFUND had 23 investment commitments in 16 countries, totalling $40 million in equity, loans or guarantees. Five to six new commitments are made annually.

Joint venture partners are determined by FINNFUND. The aim is to combine Finnish entrepreneurs' resources with local resource needs. FINNFUND concentrates on medium– and small–scale industrial companies. The Finnish partner is expected to provide technical and managerial know–how on a long–term basis. The local partner is expected to contribute local know–how and equity. To be eligible a project should be a profitable enterprise in the industrial, service or related sectors, and fit into the host–country development plan. Approval of the project by the host–country government is required.

If FINNFUND acquires shares in a joint venture, it is usually a minority participation which does not exceed that of the Finnish partner. A typical pattern is 20 per cent each for FINNFUND and the Finnish business, and 60 per cent for the host–country partner. Once the joint venture is self–sustaining, FINNFUND's mission is considered completed and its shares may be offered to the other partners. FINNFUND usually reserves the right to nominate a member to the enterprise's board of directors. In specific cases FINNFUND can participate in financial arrangements led by a local development finance institution or investment bank. FINNFUND may also acquire shares in these institutions.

Other Official Support

FINNFUND also participates in financing project preparation and feasibility studies. In general, the firm's financing share should be at least 30 per cent of the cost of the study. Financing is provided to the project on a risk basis, with a possible repayment obligation of FINNFUND's share. If the preparatory study leads to the establishment of a joint venture, the costs of the study are charged to the project. Special funds are also available on a grant basis for essential training, management and other technical assistance.

G. France

Exchange Control

The legal and administrative treatment of French outward direct investment differs as between the Franc Area countries and other countries:

a) French residents are free to invest in the Franc Area without prior authorisation. Guaranteed convertibility of currency is one of the most powerful incentives to private investment, and from this point of view the structure of the Franc Area provides effective encouragement. The currencies issued by the Central Bank of the Central African States and by the Central Bank of the West African States are defined in terms of the French franc and guaranteed by the French Treasury. Transfers are therefore not only free inside the Franc Area, but also benefit from an exchange guarantee.

b) Direct investment transfers to EEC member countries require prior notification to the Ministry of Economics and Finance.

c) Direct investment transfers exceeding FF. 1 million per year to other countries require official authorisation and have to be financed from foreign sources.

Bilateral Investment Protection Agreements

A Multilateral Convention on the Fundamental Rights of Nationals was signed in 1960 between France, Senegal, Madagascar, the Central African Republic, Congo (People's Republic of), Chad, and Gabon. This agreement is supplemented by bilateral conventions. A Convention of Establishment was signed with Togo in 1963 and a Co–operation Agreement with Mali in 1962.

Bilateral agreements on investment protection have been signed with the following countries: Tunisia, Zaire, Mauritius, Indonesia, Haiti, Yugoslavia, Egypt, South Korea, Malaysia, Morocco, Singapore, Philippines, Malta, Romania, Jordan, Syria, Sudan, Paraguay, Liberia and Sri Lanka. Negotiations are in progress with several other countries.

Investment Guarantee Scheme

As an incentive to set up establishments which are of definite benefit to the French economy, the Ministry for Economics and Finance operates a system of official guarantees against political risks. Applications are considered and decided upon individually, and it is essential that the operations to which they relate should not already have been carried out. The guarantee system consists of two distinct procedures:

— The first, managed by the BFCE[12], is a general scheme designed to encourage the growth of French industrial establishments, services and know–how abroad. Guarantees are given contingent upon the results of an analysis of the justification of the project and its various direct and indirect consequences for the French economy, usually on the assumption of a long–term involvement of the French investor.

— The other, managed by COFACE[13], is designed to encourage "export–generating" investments, i.e., those which rapidly bring about a significant increase in exports of French goods or services. Its provisions are more advantageous, but they are contingent upon the investors' commitment to an export programme, with the application of a scale of penalties if not carried out.

The two schemes are legally similar but differ significantly in the criteria on which the guarantees are given, and in the levels of cost and coverage. At the end of 1981 the total amount of investment covered was $378 million, of which BFCE held $260 million and COFACE $118 million.

The following features are common to both schemes:

a) BFCE and COFACE act as managers on behalf of the French government.

b) Guarantees are extended on a case–by–case basis, considering the benefit of each investment project to the French economy, decided by the Minister for Economics and Finance on the advice of an inter–Ministerial body.

c) Only new investments, i.e., those not yet completed when the application is made, can qualify.

d) The notion of new investment includes the creation of a production potential, the expansion of an existing one, or a new participation in an existing enterprise.

e) Detailed conditions for the guarantees and the rules governing their implementation are laid down at the outset for a fixed period (though there may be a review of a project which has developed in the interim).

f) Guarantees are expressed in French francs on the basis of the amount transferred at the time the investment is made (amounts in foreign currencies are converted into francs at the rates ruling on the date of the transfer). The coverage is therefore related not to the value of assets held abroad but to the amount of capital committed. Indemnification in case of loss may not, however, exceed the net asset value of the investment before the occurrence of the events which gave rise to the claim.

g) Transfers may be made in cash or in kind under certain conditions.

h) Transfers covered are usually those made for the purpose of subscribing capital. But, by extension, guarantees may also apply to issue premiums, blocked accounts and long–term loans by share–holders, payments to a branch or agency, or guarantees given by investors to cover long–term loans by third parties insofar as such financing or undertakings are in the nature of the investment, a question which is decided in each individual case.

i) Guarantees become effective immediately after the related transfers are made.

j) Within limits, profits reinvested or eligible for repatriation may be covered.

k) Investors must be French. This does not necessarily mean that an enterprise is not eligible for a guarantee if a part of its capital is owned by an individual or firm from a third country. Inquiries will be made, in particular, into their status as principals.

l) Guarantees relate only to claims arising directly out of political acts. Insofar as they are the direct consequence of such acts, claims are met when any of the following risks materialises:

— Interference with property: impossibility of exercising rights attached to the investment, destruction or reduction in value of the assets of the foreign enterprise, impossibility of conducting its business normally;

— Non–payment: impossibility of obtaining payment for ceding the investment, for liquidation, compensation in case of expropriation, or for any dividends covered;

— Non–transfer: impossibility of transferring outside the country the amounts due as above.

The special features of the scheme managed by BFCE are as follows:

a) Applications for guarantees require a decision by the Minister for Economics and Finance on the advice of a special inter–Ministerial committee under the chairmanship of the Director of the Treasury, known as the Grants Committee for Treasury Guarantees for French Investments Abroad (Comité d'octroi de la garantie du Trésor aux investissements français à l'étranger). The files have to be deposited with the BFCE which investigates issues and manages guarantees that have been approved. The guarantees are in the material form of a "Contrat de Garantie" signed between BFCE and the investor.

b) The operation must be of benefit to the French economy. This is appraised on the basis of the direct and indirect effects shown by an analysis over time of the submitted investment programme. The appraisal is not only in terms of immediate activity but may also take account of the international dimension which the planned establishment can secure for the French enterprise concerned, and of its contribution to spreading the reputation of French techniques throughout the world. Conversely, an investment with no noteworthy positive effect on the French economy cannot receive a guarantee.

c) The investment must be approved by the authorities of the foreign country which may have secured an agreement with France on the protection of investments or be linked with the French Treasury by an operations account (African France Area). A number of other countries are also eligible by derogation.

d) Guarantees may be given to direct investments in almost all sectors: manufacturing industry, engineering, services (insurance, transport, tourism) marketing, and so on. They are refused in principle for the following sectors:

- Oil exploration (though they may be granted for the development of oil fields and to petro–industries);
- Agriculture (though they may be granted for industries processing or marketing agricultural products);
- Real estate (though they may be granted for hotel investments);
- Financial holdings (though they may be granted for participation of financial institutions when they serve as substitute for the industrial investors).

e) Indirect investment through a holding company or temporary bridging operations carried out by a financial institution on account of the principal investor can also be covered.

f) Detailed conditions for the guarantee are fixed in each case by the Director of the Treasury on the advice of the Grants Committee. In principle there is no lower or upper limit to the percentage or amount of participation in the foreign enterprise. The Committee appraises the nature and advisability of the investment mainly from the standpoint of the control which it gives the French investor over the activities of the subsidiary. Investments which are made before an application file is lodged with BFCE, or which are to finance the participation of a local associate, do not in principle qualify for guarantees. Guarantees may be extended, on a case–by–case basis, to profits for reinvestment (capitalisation) or for repatriation (dividends) with cumulative limits of 50 per cent and 25 per cent of the initial investment respectively. The application for a guarantee must be made before the amounts are allocated, and must accompany the original application.

g) The proportion guaranteed, i.e., the percentage of the loss which is indemnified in the event of a claim, is normally 90 per cent. The Committee may, however, fix a lower proportion, depending on the details of the file. In some cases, for investments of exceptional interest to the French economy, the fraction may be higher, though it may not exceed 95 per cent. The investor must not obtain other guarantees for the remaining percentage of uncovered risk.

h) Guarantees take effect from the time at which the related transfers are made. The duration of a guarantee is decided by the Committee according to the characteristics of the investment, in particular its economic depreciation. It may not exceed fifteen years. Where an investment is carried out over a period of time, however, the starting date for measuring the duration may be the mid–point of the transfers, provided that the total duration does not exceed seventeen years.

i) There is no scaling–down of the amounts guaranteed in the last years of the guarantee period in countries which have agreed upon an investment protection convention with France or are linked with the French Treasury by an operations account. In the case of investments in countries which are eligible by derogation, however, the maximum amount guaranteed in each of the last three years of the period is in principle reduced to 75 per cent, 66 per cent and 50 per cent respectively, of the amount initially covered.

j) The commission payable annually in advance by the beneficiary for a guarantee is calculated on the basis of the capital sum invested and guaranteed (after deduction of the non–guaranteed percentage). The annual rate is normally 0.7 per cent for investments covered by an investment protection convention between the foreign country and France or made in countries linked with the

French Treasury by an operations account. It is between 0.8 per cent and 0.9 per cent in other cases, depending on the degree of protection given to the investment by the authorities of the foreign country. In exceptional cases it may be as high as 1 per cent (a distinction being made, in particular, between investments covered by a national investment code or other favourable unilateral provisions). If an investment is of particular interest for French exports but does not meet the conditions required for eligibility to the COFACE scheme described below, all or part of the provisions applying to "export generating" investments may be applied.

k) In the event of a claim, the beneficiary is indemnified if the risk was the direct consequence of one of the following acts:

— Measures taken by the foreign authorities with the deliberate intention to prejudice the investor's interests because of his nationality;

— An act or decision of the foreign authorities (nationalisation, expropriation, confiscation, sequestration);

— Violation by those authorities of any specific actions by them concerning the investment (acts recognised only within the limits fixed in each case);

— War, civil war, revolution or rioting in the foreign country;

— General moratorium declared by the foreign authorities;

— Political events or economic difficulties arising, or legislative or administrative measures taken, outside France resulting in non–transferability.

l) Industrial investments in the mining sector may benefit from more favourable conditions:

— Application may be considered for any country, and it has already been indicated that OECD countries are eligible;

— The percentage of cover may be 95 per cent;

— The duration may be of 20 years;

— There is no scaling down of the guarantee, for any country;

— The commission, settled according to the risk, is as moderate as possible in the normal range.

Generally speaking, applications concerning mining investments are investigated in a flexible way, in order to find solutions adapted to their specificity.

The special features of the scheme for "export–generating" investments managed by COFACE are described below:

a) Applications for guarantees are submitted for decision by the Minister for Economics and Finance on the advice of the Commission des Garanties et du Crédit au Commerce Extérieur ("Guarantees Committee") under the chairmanship of the Director of External Economic Relations (Direction des Relations Economiques Extérieures). Files have to be submitted by investors with the COFACE, which investigates them and issues and manages the guarantees resulting from a favourable decision. These guarantees are in the form of an insurance policy signed between COFACE and the investor.

b) The applicant must be able to demonstrate that the planned investment will bring about an increase in French exports in a way corresponding to one of the three following cases (multiplying factors):

First case: The operation results in a net current flow of additional French exports (compared with those which could normally be expected if the investment had not been made) totalling at least 3.5 times the amount of the initial capital transfers for the guaranteed investment, during the first five years following the date of the investment. This current flow must not include supplies and equipment needed for the local physical investment, and it is taken at its net value, i.e., less any additional imports into France resulting from the operation. Exports may be excluded if the greater part of their value consists of imports.

Second case: The basic supplies and services of French origin required to carry out the local physical investment represent at least 6.7 times the amount of the initial capital tranfers for the guaranteed investment (i.e., the amount of the initial tranfers to be guaranteed does not exceed 15 per cent of the amount of the exports resulting from the investment).

Third case: The operation is not eligible in accordance with either of the two cases above but the cumulative total of the two types of exports (initial supplies to carry out the local physical investment plus the net current flow) over the first five years exceeds 8 times the amount of the initial capital transfers for the guaranteed investment.

If the operation is carried out by several French investors acting in common, the transfers taken into account in these calculations are in principle those made with respect to the total initial French share in the investment. There is no geographical restriction save in exceptional circumstances, and all investments are eligible if they meet the conditions regarding their link with exports.

c) Details and conditions for the guarantee are fixed in each case by the Director of External Economic Relations on the advice of the Guarantees Committee, in accordance with its appraisal in terms of the conditions for eligibility set out above, and on the basis of the investor's undertaking as to the export programme submitted.

d) In principle, there is no lower or upper limit to the percentage or amount of participation in the foreign enterprise. The essential point is that the percentage and manner of French participation shall ensure that the export programme as submitted is realistic. In principle, any transfers made before the filing of the application with COFACE do not qualify for a guarantee. Guarantees may extend to profits for reinvestment (capitalisation) or for repatriation (dividends) within cumulative limits of 100 per cent and 50 per cent respectively of the amount of the initial investment. The application for a guarantee must be made before their allocation.

e) The proportion covered may be as high as 95 per cent depending on the characteristics of the operation. The investor must not obtain other guarantees for the remaining percentage of the risk.

f) Guarantees take effect from the time at which the related transfers are made, and their duration may not exceed 15 years. The period is measured from the date of the transfers if they are all made at the same time, or if they are made in succession, from the date on which the total transferred reaches one–half of the planned investment. However, the duration may subsequently be extended by another five years, but no more than a total of 20 years, if the investor commits himself to an export programme during these five years which represents at least five times the initial annual export programme.

g) There is no scaling–down of the amounts guaranteed in the last few years of the guarantee period.

h) The annual premium payable, calculated on the basis of the capital sum invested and guaranteed (after deduction of the non–guaranteed percentage) is 0.4 per cent. If, however, the investment is being made in a country where there are special risks and which has not entered into an investment protection convention with France, the premium may vary between 0.5 per cent and 0.6 per cent.

i) In the event of a claim, the beneficiary is indemnified if the risk was the direct consequence of one of the acts qualifying for indemnification under the BFCE scheme, or one of the following acts:

— Changes in the legislation of the foreign country concerning foreign investment;

— Sudden and unforeseeable closing of the market in the foreign country to the exports whose expansion the investment was designed to encourage.

j) The conditions of eligibility provide that the investor must submit a proposal outlining the export impact of his investment. This programme, submitted while the application file is being examined, is then incorporated into the special conditions of the insurance policy. Supervision of its execution is accompanied by a scale of penalties. For this purpose investment evaluation is carried out in two stages: a preliminary examination after three years, and a decision after five years. The scale of penalties is as follows:

— If the amount of exports is not less than 80 per cent of the forecast the guarantee is maintained;

— If it is between 50 and 80 per cent of the forecast, but nonetheless enables the minimum multiplying factor to be attained, the amount of reinvested or repatriable profits guaranteed is reduced by between 25 and 50 per cent;

— If it is below 50 per cent of the forecast, or if the minimum multiplying factor cannot be attained, the fraction covered is reduced by 10 per cent (12 per cent in case of claims arising during the first five years). The premium is increased to 0.9 per cent and the amount of reinvested or repatriable profits guaranteed is reduced by 50 per cent;

— If the exports taken into account do not equal twice the amount of the investment the guarantee is withdrawn (except in a case of exceptional circumstance or on the reasoned advice of the administration).

Fiscal Measures

So far as tax incentives to investment are concerned, relations between France and the developing countries are such that the latter fall into five groups:

First group: Countries with which there are no tax conventions. Straightforward application of French tax laws, and the rules of territoriality in particular, differ for firms and individuals:

a) Profits made outside France by firms subject to company tax are not liable for French taxation when made by a subsidiary or branch established abroad. Losses incurred outside France in the same circumstances are not deductible from profits eligible for tax in France. However, French firms investing abroad with a view to setting up a sales establishment or a research or information office, either directly or through a subsidiary, may include among their costs deductible for tax purposes an amount equal to the losses suffered during the first five years of operation of such establishment or subsidiary, up to the limit of the capital invested during those years. (The deductible amount may in certain cases equal the amount of capital invested during the first five years.) In addition, French firms making an industrial investment in developing countries, either directly or through a subsidiary, may, with the approval of the Minister for Economics and Finance, qualify for a tax–free reserve which may not, however, exceed one–half of the capital invested during these first five years of operations. Deductions in these circumstances must be added in equal parts to taxable profits during the five financial years following the first five years of operations. Finally, dividends distributed by foreign subsidiaries of French companies benefiting from the tax regulations applying to the parent company are taxable in France only for 5 per cent of their amount.

b) Profits made by individuals or partnerships liable for personal income tax are taxable in France, whatever the origin of the profits, so long as such individuals or partnerships have their main residence or place of business in France. Profits arising abroad are taxed in France, however, only up to the net amount of any tax that may have been paid abroad.

The provisions for encouraging the setting up of sales establishments or research or information offices outside France also apply to undertakings in the form of individuals or partnerships liable for personal income tax.

Second group: Guinea, Viet Nam, Cambodia, and Laos. The French regulations which traditionally apply to these countries is in the form of a system of "fiscal neutrality" whereby the French tax authorities allow tax on distributed profits collected in the host countries to be deducted from French tax payable on dividends arising in those countries.

Third group: The French Overseas Territories, the Black African States and Madagascar, Algeria and Tunisia. These States are linked to France by bilateral tax conventions designed to eliminate double taxation. So far as income from securities is concerned these conventions provide for flat–rate tax relief varying from country to country, increased in inverse proportion to the amount of tax collected locally. The effect of these incentives is to confer a yield on capital invested in securities in those countries that is higher than would be obtained in countries not linked to France by a tax convention, and generally more advantageous than that which would result from mere elimination of double taxation.

Fourth group: Certain developing countries outside the Franc area, with which conventions of a special type have been established (Israel, India, Lebanon, Pakistan, Iran, Singapore, Malaysia and the Philippines). As a general rule, these conventions avoid double taxation for French investors and enable them to retain the tax benefits which the states in this group allow to foreign investors, particularly with respect to income from securities (matching credit, sparing tax).

Fifth group: Special tax arrangements encourage private investment in the French Overseas Departments including the acquisition of land.

Official Financial Support for Private Investment

a) *The Caisse Centrale de Coopération Economique (CCCE)*[14]

Though mainly concerned with official aid, the role of the Caisse Centrale de Coopération Economique in private financing is an important one.

Its direct support of French private investment mainly takes the form of medium-term rediscount credits, long-term loans and to a very small extent, the taking of holdings in enterprises. Furthermore, the CCCE works in close co-operation with development banks in developing countries. It takes holdings in the capital of these banks and makes loans to them to enable them to participate in financing local enterprise, both public and private. It plays an important part in preparing and supervising projects financed in this way.

Since 1963 the Caisse Centrale has worked out various formulas which allow a broad association of French and local private capital in financing projects. This has been achieved in particular by coupling its long-term loans with either medium-term bank credits, which are rediscountable with overseas issuing institutes or with payment facilities provided by suppliers benefiting from credit insurance. In order to allow wider recourse to medium-term bank credit, the Caisse Centrale has on various occasions agreed to allow grace periods of as much as 5 years for the repayment of its loans. A certain number of private enterprises have thus succeeded in carrying out private investment projects using a financing formula consisting, in addition to their own funds, of about one-third long-term credits from the Caisse Centrale.

Loans by the Caisse Centrale to private enterprises in the African and Malagasy States (EAM) are only a small part of the total funds lent by the Caisse Centrale to foreign states and go mainly to industry. In recent years the Caisse Centrale has tried to intervene for the benefit of three sectors, in particular, that are of special importance to development: food crops, agro-industry and productive capital equipment.

b) *The Fonds d'Aide et de Coopération (FAC)*

The Fonds d'Aide et de Coopération (FAC) makes grants to public or semi-public bodies to enbable them to take holdings in the capital of companies contributing to the development of the African and Malagasy States (e.g., Bureau de Recherches Géologiques et Minières). FAC action in favour of private initiative also takes the form of loans for the partial financing of preinvestment studies and contributions to vocational training programmes. Finally, the FAC takes direct part in the establishment of industrial units by special very long-term loans known as "second-rank loans" made to the promoting company. These special loans, the repayment of which is deferred until after all other lenders have been paid off, may be treated as funds owned by the enterprise concerned.

c) *Union pour le Financement et l'Expansion du Commerce International (UFINEX)*

Loans for financing investment abroad may be obtained from the UFINEX company which obtains its funds by means of government-guaranteed bond issues. It grants credits for maximum periods of 15 years. Approximately 25 per cent of its loans are for investments in the developing countries. UFINEX only takes part in investment operations that will generate a volume of French exports three to four times greater than the initial investment, within a five-year period. The proportion lent varies between 50 and 100 per cent of the amount of the investment.

d) *Développement Industriel à l'Etranger (DIE)*

Since 1972 the Crédit National has extended loans, in conjunction with the BFCE, under what is known as the "DIE" procedure, to finance industrial and commercial investment abroad. Approximately one–half of the operations concern developing countries.

Information and Promotion Programme

In 1963 the Secretariat of State for Co–operation set up a Consultative Committee on industrialisation and equipment in the African and Malagasy States. Studies have been made under the auspices of this Committee with the participation of representatives of the public authorities concerned, overseas investors and French exporters to discover and decide on suitable measures for promoting industrial investment in the African and Malagasy States. In these countries the Fund for Aid and Co–operation can bear up to 50 per cent of the cost of market research, feasibility studies and engineering surveys. Furthermore, the growing contributions of the FAC to vocational training programmes are partly designed to enable private companies to obtain the intermediate and technical management essential to the achievement of development projects.

H. Germany

Exchange Control

Direct investment abroad by German residents is free from restrictions, but the Bundesbank and the Federal Ministry of Economics must be notified of each transaction for statistical purposes.

Bilateral Investment Protection Agreements

By the end of 1987, Germany had signed about 60 treaties with developing countries. With these instruments, each contracting party encourages and protects capital investments made by firms from the other party. Foreign investors are thus guaranteed fair and equitable treatment (in particular, national treatment and application of the most favoured nation clause). Their investments are protected against unjustified expropriation and against expropriation without adequate and prompt compensation.

Other provisions normally contained in German investment promotion and protection treaties are:

— Free transfer of the invested capital, earnings, and liquidation proceeds at the current exchange rate;
— Arbitration procedures for dispute settlement;
— The treaty is valid for ten years but will remain in force unless revoked;
— If the treaty is revoked, the provisions remain in force for investments made before the date of revocation for a further twenty–year period.

The German business community considers these treaties and agreements as a generally useful contribution to a good investment climate. Experience has shown that host countries shy away from even minor breaches of their international obligations once an agreement has been signed. Host countries do not wish to lose standing in the international business community. The network of such treaties and agreements, several of which were concluded in the early 1960s, continues to expand. Recent treaties were concluded with Bolivia and Uruguay.

Investment Guarantee Scheme

German direct investments in developing countries can be protected against political risks by official guarantees issued under a scheme which was established in 1960. To be eligible for a guarantee, an investment must satisfy the following tests:

— It must be new;
— It must have positive effects on the economies of both the host country and Germany;
— The situation for foreign investment in the host country must appear satisfactory at the time of approval, with respect to legal protection against political risks. This is assumed to be the case in countries with which investment protection treaties or agreements are in force. No new guarantees can be approved for investment in countries where claims under the guarantee scheme are pending.

The types of investment that can be guaranteed are i) equity, ii) loans provided to foreign enterprises in which the creditor also holds equity and iii) donation or endowment capital to overseas branches of German enterprises.

The guarantee covers the usual political risks:

— Expropriation, nationalisation and similar, politically motivated official measures;
— War, revolution;
— Impossibility of transferring capital and earnings.

The coverage offered by the guarantee is limited to 95 per cent of incurred loss. Reinvested earnings up to 300 per cent of the covered original investment may be included in the guarantee. Remitted earnings that have not yet been transferred are covered to the extent of 10 per cent of the investment annually and up to 50 per cent in total. Guarantees last fifteen years, but their duration can be extended for another five years. The costs for the German investor of the guarantee is a one–time inscription fee of between 0.05 and 0.1 per cent and an annual fee of 0.5 per cent of the guaranteed amount. New forms of foreign investment, replacing equity participation, that have been developed in the petroleum sector, e.g., service contracts and production sharing agreements, can also be protected against political risks by the German guarantee scheme. This guarantee, introduced in 1977, concerns the contractor's claim to be refunded for exploration and development costs as well as his option of buying petroleum from wells developed by him. In these cases, however, the coverage is limited to 70 per cent of the capital amount invested.

Applications for guarantees are processed by a private corporation, Treuarbeit[15], acting on behalf of the government. After considering each project, an inter–ministerial committee composed of representatives of the Ministries for Economics, Finance, Foreign Affairs and Economic Co–operation decides whether to approve the guarantee for a given project. At the end of 1987, about 2 400 applications for Federal Investment Guarantees for developing countries (DAC classification) had been approved, with total investment being about 8.3 billion DM (approximatly $4.4 billion).

Fiscal Measures

By the end of 1987, 40 bilateral agreements for the avoidance of double taxation had been completed or signed with developing countries. While such agreements commonly adopt the principle of residence as a basis of taxation, the German agreements with developing countries increasingly apply the principle of taxation in the source country. Thus, tax holidays or exemptions granted by a developing country are treated as (fictitious) tax credits deductible from the investor's tax liabilities in Germany. In the absence of a double taxation agreement, a similar outcome is achieved by the provisions of the Foreign Taxation Act.

A special law on Tax Measures for Foreign Investments of German Industry, passed in 1969, is applicable to ventures in both developing and developed countries. Under certain conditions it allows the investor to create profit–reducing reserves or to deduct losses incurred by his foreign venture from his domestic profits.

The Public Investment Corporation, DEG[16]

The German Finance Company for Investments in Developing Countries (DEG) was founded in 1962 with the aim of supporting and encouraging German entrepreneurs, in particular of medium and small scale enterprises, to establish branches or affiliates in developing countries. DEG's authorised capital, currently DM 1 billion, is fully held by the Federal Government. The DEG is a non–profit institution, but operates on normal business principles to the extent that this is compatible with its general objectives. The Federal Government does not interfere with the selection of the individual projects, but is represented on the supervisory board, together with a majority of representatives from German business. The DEG usually operates in partnership arrangements with a German partner and a partner from the developing host country in the form of joint ventures. The Company actively seeks new investment opportunities and makes proposals to German industry and trade. It helps German firms establish local contacts and find local partners, and advises businessmen on operating conditions in developing countries. The financial contribution consists of equity participation or loans with equity features. Investments supported by the Company must benefit the economic development of the host country. Particular emphasis is laid on transfer of private capital, managerial and technological know–how, processing of local raw materials, improvement of balance of payments and the creation of permanent jobs. The projects must fit into the economic structure and development plan of the host country and must be approved by the host country government. "Co–ordinated projects", in which official aid is combined with private investment, can also be supported. Twenty–three per cent of DEG funds is invested in national (either state or privately owned) development financing institutions. The DEG thus participates indirectly in the financing of additional projects in various countries.

The DEG offers German enterprises of medium size (annual turnover of up to DM 50 million) which intend to invest in developing countries a particular funding programme. Funds of this programme, depending on the developmental importance of the intended investment, may be available to enterprises with an annual turnover of up to DM 300 million. For craft enterprises and small industries (annual turnover up to DM 12 million) an additional financing programme on even more favourable conditions is made available (Chamber of Commerce Programme). Since the introduction of the small and medium enterprise programme in 1983 and the Chamber of

Commerce Programme in 1986, a total of 87 investments have drawn on these special financing programmes.

The DEG made commitments of about DM 1.8 billion to a total of 420 enterprises between 1962 and the end of 1987. In 1987, the DEG committed some DM 147 million for 64 projects in 32 countries.

Since the Company's leverage depends largely on the number of new projects it can help to start, the DEG is interested in terminating its participation in any given project as soon as this seems possible. In selling its participation to the partners, the Company obtains funds for new investments.

Promotion of Business Co-operation

In view of the fact that small and medium-sized companies suffer from a major lack of experience in co-operating with enterprises in developing countries, the German Government initiated in 1984 the Programme for the Promotion of Business Co-operation (the BC Programme), an advisory service for industry in developing countries. Designed to complement investment guarantee schemes, fiscal measures, credit aid, equity investments and promotion of training, the BC Programme provides practical aid by establishing contacts and identifying partners. The services include:

— Specialised management consultancy on joint ventures, transfer of technical and business know-how, and development of new markets on the basis of long-term co-operation agreements with companies in the Federal Republic of Germany and developing countries;
— Advisory services to the responsible national bodies in developing countries in creating an environment conducive to private sector development.

The nucleus of the BC Programme is the BC consulting team, which implements all business co-operation activities between a particular developing country and the Federal Republic of Germany. One member of this team is based in the BC promotion office in the developing country, usually attached to an organisation representing the private sector, or an official investment/export promotion centre, or a development bank or similar relevant organisation. The other team member is based in the Federal Republic of Germany, where he is responsible for the BC Programme for the developing country concerned. There are at present 32 advisers in the developing countries and 26 in the Federal Republic of Germany trying to establish co-operation between enterprises. In 1986, they handled more than one thousand prospective cases of co-operation, and some 250 have come to fruition. The German Agency for Technical Co-operation (GTZ) and the German Finance Company for Investments in Developing Countries (DEG) are the executive agencies for the programme. This programme has been reviewed and may be expanded into a broader advisory service package covering production and marketing problems of firms in developing countries, policy questions at government level, and advice to institutions such as chambers of commerce and industries and export councils.

In addition to the BC Programme, a number of investment advisory services, both official and private, provide information on investment opportunities for German industry, including general information on the investment climate, changes of legislation, etc., in various developing countries. The Federal Agency for Foreign Trade Information[17], supervised by the Ministries for Economics and Foreign Affairs, is an important institution here. As far as private institutions are concerned, German enterprises interested in ventures in developing countries may request information from one of the four

"Landervereine" in Hamburg (associations of trading companies dealing with Africa, Latin America, East Asia and the Middle East, respectively), or from the Association of German Industry (BDI) in Cologne, or from the Confederation of German Chambers of Industry and Commerce (DIHT) in Bonn.

Other Financial Support for Foreign Direct Investment

A financial support programme, "Subsidiary Companies Programme", set up in 1979 to promote the establishment of German subsidiaries in developing countries (replacing the previous ERP subsidiary scheme), had provided 428 commitments of DM 307 million for enterprises in 56 countries by 31st December 1987. The official loans are extended at highly favourable terms: fifteen years maturity (including a five–year grace period), 2.5 per cent interest for investments in the least developed countries and 3.5 per cent in other developing countries. This programme is a useful addition to the existing instruments for promoting the activities of the private sector in developing countries. In conjunction with official investment guarantees and DEG participation, it is helping to increase the level of investment by German enterprises, even in the higher–risk developing countries.

The "Technology Programme" was created to promote the economic application of new technologies by German enterprises in developing countries. The programme was designed to help transfer German firms' technologies to developing countries through joint ventures. The programme reduces the risks of introducing new technologies in the developing countries by providing loans to German enterprises at particularly favourable terms. The loans have a maturity period of up to fifteen years, including a grace period of not more than five years. During the grace period the interest is one per cent per annum, thereafter 2.5 per cent per annum. The size of the loan amounts to 50 per cent of the finance raised by the German firm; in cases involving substantial technological and financial risk, it can be more. The maximum loan amount of DM 2 500 000 can also be exceeded in exceptional cases. The loans can be used to finance the costs of setting up production, including management costs, training local personnel, and technological overhaul and renewal of production methods. The programme's favourable loan terms (and the possibility that the obligation to repay the loan can be waived) are intended as incentives to small and medium–sized German firms to transfer to the developing countries technologies which have not yet been introduced there, and make possible the production of goods which these countries need. Up to December 1987, a total of 78 loans were extended, totalling DM 106 million.

I. Italy

Policy to promote direct investment flows to the developing countries

To foster favourable conditions for bilateral private investment, Italy has signed or is in the process of negotiating several agreements on investment safeguards with developing countries. Industrial economic co–operation agreements often include specific clauses on direct investment.

It has already been possible to conclude a number of agreements in Africa (Egypt, Tunisia) and Asia (China, Malaysia, Sri Lanka) and negotiations are proceeding with such countries as Thailand, Indonesia and South Korea.

These investment agreements have been accompanied by agreements on double taxation.

Under Law No. 49/87, promoting private investment in the Third World has become one of the policy objectives of Italy's bilateral development assistance programme. It is part of the strategy to foster the development of local production capacity, and to strengthen the private sector.

Strategy with respect to the private sector is based on the following measures:

a) Section 7 of Law No. 49/87 authorising the use of public funds to finance joint ventures;

b) Programmes to promote the development of small and medium–sized enterprises (SMEs), notably in Argentina, Uruguay and Tunisia;

c) Support for multilateral bodies working in this area (IFC, the regional development banks, UNDP programmes such as the one to promote SMEs in Africa, etc.);

d) Increased technical assistance (not yet fully developed) to support local SME management.

Measures to promote direct investment in the developing countries under the new Law on Development Co–operation No. 49/87

Section 7 of the new law states that financial assistance will be provided through the granting of concessional loans to Italian enterprises, with partial financing of their share of the risk capital of joint ventures to be established in developing countries.

The law would seem to favour joint ventures for two reasons: not only are they politically more acceptable in the country of investment, they are also the instrument most commonly used by the Italian entrepreneurs active in this sector.

The facility provided under Section 7 of the new law on co–operation is set out in a memorandum of the Steering Committee for Development Co–operation dated 10th July 1987, which in fact constitutes the instructions concerning Section 7 of the law. This facility may be summarised as follows:

— Inasmuch as the financing of joint ventures is part of development assistance policy, preference will be given (though not exclusively) to projects in agriculture and industry. Projects in designated priority countries for Italian development co–operation, and those where local financing accounts for over 50 per cent of invested capital will also receive priority;

— Financing will be granted for a maximum of ten years, with a grace period of up to two years from start–up, and carry an interest rate equal to one–third of the reference rate set by the Treasury Ministry (around 9 per cent in July 1988);

— Financing may not exceed L 20 billion for any given project. The contribution may be up to 70 per cent of the Italian venture capital for an amount not exceeding the first L 10 billion tranche of equity participation, and up to 50 per cent of the part over and above that limit;

— Projects will be subjected to technical appraisal by the Directorate General for Development Co–operation and an appraisal of their banking and financial aspects by the Mediocredito Centrale;

— Concessional credit will be granted by decree of the Treasury Ministry on the recommendation of the Ministry for Foreign Affairs. It will be disbursed by the Mediocredito Centrale on the basis of a financing contract between the Mediocredito and the enterprise involved;

— Commitment guarantees may also be provided on the basis of a preliminary feasibility study.

Criteria for applying measures to promote direct investment

Since the system is still at the start–up stage, it is difficult to describe the actual criteria that should be applied in connection with the new financial instrument. Probably only after a period of some years will it be possible to identify, on the basis of trial and error and daily use, the most appropriate general principles for building investment financing into the development co–operation policy as a whole. Nevertheless, even at the present time some general criteria clearly emerge:

a) In preparing investment projects it will certainly be useful to focus not only on the financial, commercial and technical aspects of the investment itself, but also on the effective transfer of management capability by the Italian enterprise to the joint venture; it is likely that priority will go to projects for which the Italian entrepreneur can demonstrate a direct commitment in terms of administration and management, which are often the weak points of developing–country enterprises;

b) There will obviously be a need in the joint venture scheme to ensure an appropriate ratio of venture capital to debt. It will probably not be possible to define a theoretical ratio valid in all circumstances, since the ratio will differ according to investment content and other contingent factors, but it would clearly be difficult to establish a joint venture which is underfunded in relation to loan capital;

c) Last, consideration must be given to the possibility of using new venture capital financing in conjunction with other financial instruments.

In safeguarding direct investment against political risk, it is best to insure Italian participation in the joint venture with the SACE (as provided for under Law 227).

Under Italian development co–operation policy, it is not only venture capital facilities that are made available for investment projects, but also ODA loans and associated financing. It is thus possible to arrange full financial packages involving financing and national and international guarantees covering both the venture capital and the loan financing aspects of the proposed joint venture.

In a longer–term perspective, Italian enterprises lacking experience in this area should ideally be provided with technical and financial assistance to help them mount such packages on the basis of the instruments available; this is a highly specialised activity, but one which could give excellent results.

Last, assistance by the Italian development co–operation authorities should not only be viewed from the angle of financial facilities. It must be remembered that these projects will be sited in countries which receive substantial Italian aid and which are constantly submitting fresh requests. Inserting a joint venture into the aid programme implies official recognition at government level, even if the enterprise is to remain in the private sector. Should problems emerge at a later stage, it may reasonably be supposed that a joint venture of this type would receive preferential treatment by the local authorities, at least compared to entirely private undertakings. This may prove to be a significant additional guarantee in countries with a high degree of state control.

J. Japan

Bilateral Investment Protection Agreements

The first investment protection agreement between Japan and a developing country was signed with Egypt in 1977, followed by a similar agreement with Sri Lanka in 1982. Japan has also ratified treaties of friendship, commerce and navigation containing clauses on the protection of private interests (remittance of profits, confiscation of property, etc.) with a number of developing countries.

Investment Guarantee Scheme

In 1970, the Japanese authorities instituted the Overseas Investment Insurance Scheme, which merged two older programmes into one and extended the scope of application. The use of the scheme by Japanese investors has increased sharply. The scheme was further improved in 1972, 1974, 1981 and 1987 and is administered by the Ministry of International Trade and Industry (MITI)[18].

The scheme covers the three principal categories of political risk (war, expropriation and exchange transfer), as well as commercial risk (bankruptcy). Regarding the transfer risk, remittance blockages must last at least two months. The scheme applies to direct investment in the form of equity, long–term loans and joint ventures (lasting five years or more, even if they are not controlled by a Japanese company), real estate, equipment, etc. It can also guarantee portfolio investment and long–term loans for an enterprise which, although not under Japanese control, is engaged in the exploitation of mineral resources. For example, enterprises producing timber and other goods to be imported by Japan under long–term supply contracts are covered under the programme. In this case, commercial risk is extended for defaulting borrowers for six months or more.

To be eligible for insurance, an investment must be made in a new project or in the expansion of an existing enterprise. The project must have a favourable effect on the host country and contribute to Japan's international economic relations. The investment climate in the host country is taken into consideration.

The scheme covers principal (100 per cent) and profits (up to 10 per cent per annum of the residual amount of investment to a maximum of 100 per cent over the contract life). The maximum period of coverage is normally fifteen years. In exceptional cases the interval between the date of the investment and the date of the start of operations may be added to that period. In the event of loss, the claim payable for political risk is 90 per cent (70 per cent for the other forms of guarantee) of the original amount of investment, or the estimated value at the time of the loss, whichever is the smaller. For commercial risk, the claim payable is 40 per cent and in the case of expropriation 80 per cent. The annual premium is 0.55 per cent for the three political risks combined and 1.25–1.55 per cent if the policy also covers commercial risk.

Total insurance liabilities outstanding at the end of 1986 amounted to more than $10 billion.

Fiscal measures

One of the basic rules of Japanese tax legislation is to grant equal treatment to domestic and foreign investment. In 1962 a more liberal method of calculating tax credit on foreign sources of income was adopted and the types of income eligible for tax credits were expanded. In 1964 a system was established for tax deferment on investments in developing countries. This measure now applies to investments made between 1st April 1973 and 31st March 1988.

Double taxation agreements have been concluded with the following countries: Brazil, China, India, Indonesia, Ireland, Korea, Malaysia (revised), Pakistan, Philippines, Singapore (revised), Spain, Sri Lanka, Thailand and Zambia.

Official Financial Support

The Japanese Government extends financial facilities to Japanese investors mainly through the Export–Import Bank of Japan[19], the Overseas Economic Cooperation Fund (OECF)[20] and the Japan International Cooperation Agency (JICA)[21].

i) Established in 1950, the Exim Bank of Japan is an institution with a great variety of activities. Its purpose is to promote financially Japan's economic interchange in such fields as plant export, development and import of natural resources, import of manufactured goods, and overseas direct investment. Also important is providing untied direct loans to developing countries for their priority projects, economic restructuring programmes, and energy development projects. Credits to support Japanese overseas direct investment also constitute an important part of the Bank's operations. Its Overseas Investment Credit facility (OIC), a long–term financing instrument, is made available to Japanese corporations and Japanese overseas joint ventures, as well as to foreign governments and financial institutions which make co-investments in developing countries without increasing their external debts. The aggregate amount of OIC commitments was approximately $1 600 million in FY 1986.

ii) Established in 1961, the OECF is an agency that primarily extends concessional official development loans (ODA loans) to the governments of developing countries. But it also supplies funds in the form of long–term soft loans for projects by Japanese enterprises if such projects promote economic development in the developing countries concerned. Funds are also available for pre–investment surveys. The annual amounts of investment credits extended by the OECF vary widely. Commitments in FY 1984 and FY 1985 were $200 million and $98 million respectively.

iii) The JICA was established in 1974. It is the executing agency for technical co–operation but it also provides finance for projects in such fields as social development, agriculture and forestry, and mining and manufacturing in developing countries (if such funds cannot be obtained from the Exim Bank of Japan or the OECF). JICA facilitates financing for infrastructure related to development projects undertaken by Japanese nationals, if such infrastructure also contributes to the development of the adjacent areas. JICA also undertakes experimental development projects which are difficult to realise unless they are carried out in combination with technical innovation or development.

iv) In addition to the three public financial institutions mentioned above, the Japan Petroleum Development Corporation, and the Metal Mining Agency of Japan, both public corporations, supply funds for investment abroad in the field of exploration of petroleum and other important mineral resources. Finally, the Japan Overseas Development Corporation is a semi–public corporation established in 1970 to promote industrial development and trade with developing countries. It also provides financing to Japanese firms and nationals, mainly to establish joint ventures in countries where the projects will contribute to economic development.

Other Official Support

The Japanese Government subsidises various private technical assistance activities to encourage direct investment in developing countries. For example, private organisations such as the Association for Overseas Technical Scholarships and the Japan Productivity Centre are subsidised to train participants from developing countries. Subsidies are also provided to the Engineering Consulting Firms Association for its pre-investment survey activities and to other private bodies for investment surveys. In agricultural investment, the government subsidises the Overseas Agricultural Development Association for promoting investment to agricultural projects on a commercial basis.

K. Netherlands

Exchange Control

Outward direct investment is free. Loans to foreign subsidiaries exceeding Gld. 10 million per year and per debtor are subject to prior authorisation.

Bilateral Investment Promotion and Protection Agreements

The Netherlands has entered into bilateral agreements with a number of developing countries, which, among other things, provide for the promotion and protection of private investments. Agreements have so far been secured with, Cameroon, China, Côte d'Ivoire, Egypt, Ghana, Indonesia, Kenya, Republic of Korea, Malaysia, Malta, Morocco, Oman, Pakistan, Philippines, Senegal, Singapore, Sri Lanka, Sudan, Tanzania, Thailand, Tunisia, Turkey, Uganda, Uruguay, Yemen (Arab Republic), Yugoslavia.

These agreements are characterised by the following: fair and equitable treatment, non-discrimination with respect to investments, the right of immediate transfer of profits and the repatriation of invested capital, the payment of just compensation in the event of expropriation, and provisions for subrogation and state-state as well as state-investor arbitration.

Investment Guarantee Scheme

In 1969, the Netherlands Parliament passed a bill introducing an official reinsurance scheme for non-commercial risk policies contracted between investors and Dutch banks or insurance companies designated by the Ministry of Finance.

The official reinsurance scheme is operated by a private credit insurance company, the "Nederlandse Credietverzekering Maatschappij N.V." (Netherlands Credit Insurance Company)[22]. The scheme only applies to new direct investments in developing countries and is subject to satisfactory procedural arrangements for dealing with disputes. The preliminary approval of each investment by the host country is required for individual policies. The Ministry of Finance fixed a ceiling for the guarantees which amounted to Gld. 500 million at the end of 1981.

The scheme covers the three main categories of political risks:
— Expropriation, nationalisation and similar, politically motivated official measures;
— War, revolution, etc.;
— Impossibility of transferring capital and earnings.

The scheme is being extended to cover a fourth category, breach of contract by the host government. This extension should have been operational before the end of 1989.

The coverage applies to both equity and loan investments. The initial amount insured is usually the amount of investment in Dutch guilders. A limit is fixed for maximum indemnity of principal and earnings together (in principle 150 per cent of the initial value of the investment). Untransferable earnings will be reimbursed within the above ceiling to a maximum of 8 per cent per annum of the original investment insured, applicable during the insurance year in which the revenue concerned was payable.

The maximum length of a guarantee is twenty years and in exceptional cases twenty–five years from the date of the insurance policy. This length, however, cannot exceed fifteen years from the date at which the investment was completed. After ten years of full coverage, the guarantee is reduced to 90 per cent in the eleventh year, 80 per cent in the twelfth year and so forth until the fifteenth and last year, for which the coverage is 50 per cent. The purpose of this provision is to reduce the commitments of the Netherlands Government in good time but gradually enough so as not to inconvenience the investor.

In the event of loss, at least 10 per cent would be at the expense of the investor himself. The premium for coverage against non–commercial risks is 5.5 per cent per annum of the current amount. If transfer risks are excluded it is 4.5 per cent per annum; if breach of contract is included it is 0.7 per cent per annum. These premiums are applicable when the Netherlands has concluded an investment protection agreement with the countries concerned, otherwise 0.2 per cent have to be added to the premiums. At the end of 1987 Gld. 167 million of investments in developing countries were guaranteed.

Fiscal Measures

To date, 18 bilateral tax agreements have been concluded with developing countries. In the absence of bilateral tax conventions, Dutch tax law does not generally make any distinction between income from investment in developing or industrialised countries.

Under the Unilateral Decree on the Avoidance of Double Taxation, which applies to all countries not covered by bilateral agreements, the tax levied at the source by developing countries on dividends, interest and royalties may, as a rule, be credited against the tax levied in the Netherlands thereon. If the foreign tax cannot be fully offset against the amount of Dutch tax levied in one year, the Decree allows the balance to be offset against Dutch tax on the same type of income in the eight years following the year in which the dividends, interest and royalties were received from developing countries.

The Netherlands Development Finance Company (FMO)[23]

The FMO is a Dutch development bank working especially for companies in developing countries. The Netherlands Government holds 51 per cent of its shares, and the balance is owned by the Dutch business community including employers, federations and labour unions.

The objective of the FMO is to stimulate the growth of the productive sector in developing countries by providing risk capital and/or medium– and long–term loans to local enterprises. The FMO also has a "soft window" for investment promotion and technical assistance to local enterprises, and for special programmes (through local institutions) for small enterprises. FMO finance is not tied to Dutch procurement or co–operation with Dutch enterprises.

By the end of 1988 the FMO had provided the equivalent of US$300 million to some 150 projects in 41 developing countries in Africa, Asia and Latin America. In a number of countries the FMO works in close co–operation with local development banks, to which it provides finance for onlending to local enterprises.

Investment promotion can be assisted through finance for feasibility studies and pilot projects, and technical assistance may include the financing of temporary external expertise, or sending employees for external training or education.

The FMO can be directly approached by enterprises from the Netherlands or from developing countries.

L. New Zealand

Bilateral Investment Protection Agreements

New Zealand has not signed any specific agreements with developing countries for the protection of direct investments by New Zealand companies.

Fiscal Measures

New Zealand has entered into six bilateral agreements on the avoidance of double taxation with developing countries: the Philippines, Fiji, Malaysia, India, the Republic of Korea and the People's Republic of China.

Investment Guarantee Scheme

The New Zealand Investment Guarantee Scheme, administered by the Export Guarantee Office (EXGO)[24], has provided coverage since 1973 for new equity investments in foreign enterprises against the risks of exchange transfer, expropriation and war damage. It covers 90 per cent of the initial amount of investment. Accumulated investment earnings (up to 200 per cent of the initial investment) can be covered against exchange transfer and expropriation risks. The premium for the three risks together is negotiated for each contract. The maximum duration of the coverage is fifteen years while the minimum is five years.

Development of Investment and Trade in the South Pacific

The Pacific Islands Industrial Development Scheme provides financial assistance by way of grants and loans to New Zealand businesses establishing or expanding manufacturing or processing operations or setting up agricultural ventures in the South Pacific Forum island countries. The scheme, administered by the Department of Trade and Industry, aims to foster economic development and the growth of employment opportunities in the islands concerned. The countries covered by the Scheme are: Cook Islands, Fiji, Kiribati, Nauru, Niue, Papua New Guinea, Solomon Islands, Tonga, Tuvalu, Vanuatu and Western Samoa.

The South Pacific Regional Trade and Economic Co–operation Agreement (SPARTECA) provides free access of most goods from Pacific Forum island countries to New Zealand and Australia. In addition, the SPARTECA also provides trade and economic assistance under Articles VIII and IX of the Agreement.

Within its aid programme New Zealand has a special fund administered by the Department of Trade and Industry to assist trade development. This fund targets the commercial sector of the Pacific island countries.

M.   Norway

Bilateral Investment Protection Agreements

Bilateral agreements for the protection of private investment have been signed with Indonesia, Sri Lanka, Malaysia and China.

Investment Guarantee Scheme

The operation of the Investment Guarantee Scheme has been suspended. A new scheme is at present under evaluation.

Fiscal Measures

No special treatment is provided by Norwegian tax legislation to favour income from investments in developing countries. But Norway has entered into double taxation agreements with the following developing countries: Benin, Brazil, China, Egypt, Gambia, Grenada, India, Israel, Côte d'Ivoire, Kenya, Malaysia, Malta, Morocco, Netherlands Antilles, Portugal, Pakistan, Singapore, South Korea, Spain, Sri Lanka, Tanzania, Thailand, Trinidad and Tobago, Tunisia, Turkey and Zambia.

Other Official Support

As a precondition for support, the Ministry of Development Co–operation (MDC) will seek to ensure that projects meet the developmental needs of the countries concerned. Priority will be given to projects which increase and strengthen the productive capacity of the poorer developing countries, are labour–intensive, use local raw materials, contribute to the improvement of managerial and technical skills, and have export potential. Only projects which are economically sound, financially viable, technically feasible and have competent management will be supported.

MDC provides the following incentives to stimulate private investment in developing countries.

a) Pre–investment studies carried out by the potential Norwegian investor can be supported on a reimbursable basis. MDC may finance up to 50 per cent of eligible expenses. In considering an application under this programme, MDC examines the resources (financial, managerial, personnel, technical, etc.) of the applicant which are needed to carry out the overseas project, as well as his business record in Norway in similar projects.

b) MDC can provide medium– and long–term loan finance on concessional terms, i.e., with a grant element of minimum 25 per cent (as calculated by the OECD). Equity finance cannot be provided except in certain cases where loans are given to the host government or to other public authorities or institutions to finance their part of the project. MDC will not normally finance or otherwise commit itself to any enterprise for more than 50 per cent of the project's debt financing. MDC's lending decisions will be based on appraisal methods that take into account the total financial requirements of the project and the soundness of the enterprise's financial structure. Conditions for each loan with regard to collateral, reporting and performance will be agreed on an individual basis. Loans will normally be secured by a mortgage if permitted by host country law.

c) Grants or concessional finance for basic infrastructure: when a project is located in an area where the national or local authorities are unable to finance the basic infrastructure required for project implementation, MDC can assist with loans on concessional terms or grants. Road construction, quay and harbour development, local power distribution, housing, educational institutions and health services may qualify for support. The amount of investment required, however, should not be disproportionate to the size of the project.

d) MDC can also assist by partially financing initial training schemes essential to the company's operations.

e) MDC can guarantee loans from other sources when it has proved difficult or impossible to obtain part of the basic debt financing from commercial sources. No commission will be charged for such guarantees. Exposure limits and conditions are the same as for medium– and long–term loans.

N. Sweden

Bilateral Investment Protection Agreements

Sweden has concluded bilateral investment protection agreements with eight developing countries, namely: China, Egypt, Malaysia, Pakistan, Sri Lanka, Tunisia, the Yemen Arab Republic and Yugoslavia.

Investment Guarantee Scheme

In 1987, the Swedish Parliament approved changes in the investment guarantee scheme which had been in effect since 1968. The most important change is that guarantees may be issued for investments in almost all countries. The scheme is administered by the Swedish Export Credits Guarantee Board (EKN). Guarantees may be issued up to a maximum of SKr 1 billion ($150 million).

To be eligible for a guarantee, the investment should have a positive impact on the Swedish economy. New projects and the expansion of existing facilities are eligible for guarantees. The investor should normally have substantial control over the investment. Swedish minority participation may be considered on a case–by–case basis. Financial participation as well as contributions in kind may be covered. The guarantee covers the three main categories of political risk (currency transfer, expropriation and war) and applies both to the original investment and to remitted earnings of up to 20 per cent per annum of the highest amount of investment covered at any time. The total amount of guaranteed remitted earnings, however, cannot exceed 100 per cent of the amount of the original investment. Reinvested profits are normally guaranteed on the condition that they were transferable at the time of reinvestment.

In the event of loss, the payable claim will not exceed 90 per cent of the amount covered. Moreover, compensation will not take place before the investor has appealed to the local authorities. Normally, guarantees will be issued for a limited period, not exceeding 15 years.

The guarantee fee will be set according to the country and the guarantee period.

Fiscal Measures

In principle, both the tax rates on net income and depreciation allowances are the same for domestic and foreign operations. However, unless a double taxation treaty applies, foreign tax on foreign income may under certain conditions be deducted from gross profits either as a cost, or credited against Swedish state income tax.

Twenty–two double taxation agreements have been signed with developing countries (Argentina, Bangladesh, Brazil, China, Egypt, India, Israel, Jamaica, Kenya, South Korea, Malaysia, Malta, Morocco, Pakistan, Peru, Philippines, Singapore, Sri Lanka, Thailand, Tunisia, Tanzania and Zambia). Arrangements for the avoidance of double taxation have been made with Nigeria.

As a general rule, the tax treaties with developing countries provide for proportionally higher taxation in the host country than do tax agreements between Sweden and the industrialised countries. Under a treaty with a developing country, a Swedish company will generally be exempt from Swedish income tax on dividends from a foreign subsidiary. On the other hand, if the "tax credit" method is used (as a general method or for certain types of income) Sweden has often agreed to give a credit for taxes spared in recognition of the incentives granted by the host country.

The Public Investment Corporation, SWEDFUND

The Swedish Fund for Industrial Co–operation with Developing Countries, SWEDFUND[25], which became operational in 1979, is an independent fund with an authorised capital of SKr 250 million ($40 million). The Fund is allowed to borrow three times its paid–in capital with a government guarantee.

The purpose of the SWEDFUND is to promote industrial activities in developing countries by:

a) Acting as a broker between interested parties in developing countries and the Swedish business community;

b) Financing, in part, feasibility studies; and

c) Contributing to joint ventures with equity participation and/or loans and guarantees.

SWEDFUND's total contribution in the form of equity loans and guarantees should not normally exceed 30 per cent of the total project costs.

The Fund co–operates with public as well as private partners of any size, both in Sweden and in developing countries, but with particular emphasis on small and medium–sized firms. In particular, SWEDFUND promotes projects in those countries which already have a long–standing development co–operation relationship with

Sweden, or which pursue development policies consistent with the aims and objectives established by the official Swedish development co-operation programme.

Only projects which have a favourable impact on the development of the host country and which have been approved by its government are considered. When assessing the economic impact of a project, SWEDFUND pays special attention to:

a) The creation of employment opportunities;
b) The training and education of manpower;
c) The transfer of technology and its adaptation to local conditions;
d) The foreign-exchange effects on the host country;
e) The environmental impact;
f) The degree of integration in the local economy and society.

New ventures and the expansion of existing enterprises may be considered. The exploitation of mineral and other natural resources are not eligible for SWEDFUND support unless they include a manufacturing element. Contributions by the Fund are not conditional upon Swedish equipment being purchased for the project. Active local participation is usually a prerequisite for the Fund's participation. The local participants can be manufacturing companies, investment banks, development corporations or private individuals.

Although SWEDFUND is an independent body which makes its contributions to projects on the basis of its own analysis, it works closely with the Swedish International Development Authority (SIDA) and the Swedish Agency for International Technical and Economic Co-operation (BITS).

SWEDFUND does not, as a rule, participate in projects which have a debt/equity ratio of more than 65/35. When its equity participation is no longer required, the Fund may sell its shares to other project partners, preferably those of the host country. Shareholding is not a condition for the extension of SWEDFUND loans. Loans normally have a grace period corresponding to the construction and start-up period of the project. Thereafter the loans are to be repaid over a period not exceeding ten years.

O. Switzerland

Bilateral Investment Protection Agreements

Between 1961 and 1986, bilateral agreements for the promotion and protection of investments have been signed with 20 developing countries (China, Costa Rica, Ecuador, Egypt, Honduras, Indonesia, Jordan, South Korea, Malaysia, Mali, Morocco, Panama, Singapore, Sri Lanka, Sudan, Syria, Tanzania, Tunisia, Uganda, and Zaire). Agreements on commerce, investment protection and technical co-operation have been concluded with 14 countries (Benin, Burkina Faso, Cameroon, Chad, Congo, Côte d'Ivoire, Gabon, Guinea, Madagascar, Malta, Mauritania, Niger, Senegal, Togo), and agreements on commerce and investment protection have been signed with two countries (Central African Republic, Rwanda). A friendship and commercial treaty, including a clause on investment protection has been signed with Liberia. The main provisions of these bilateral agreements are as follows:

a) A guarantee of non-discrimination in the form of a national treatment clause and a most favoured nation clause;
b) A guarantee of the transfer of investment earnings, and of the repatriation of the initial capital when the investment is terminated;

c) A guarantee against arbitrary expropriation or nationalisation, and a compensation clause providing for rapid, fair, and effective compensation to an investor who is directly or indirectly deprived of his assets;

d) Arbitration procedures.

Investment Guarantee Scheme

The Swiss scheme for the guarantee of investments in developing countries against non–commercial risk, established in 1970, is administered by the Department of Economics in agreement with the Department of Politics and Finance. The guarantee normally applies only to equity participation, but can be extended to foreign loans issued in Switzerland. Only new investments which promote the economic development of the recipient country can receive the guarantee. The limit for total government commitments under the guarantee has been fixed at SF 500 million ($330 million). Investment coverage at the end of 1986 amounted to $32 million.

The guarantee covers the three main categories of political risk. In addition, for loan capital and interest it can be extended to cover insolvency or refusal to pay on the part of governments and other public authorities. In addition to new investment, the guarantee also applies to reinvested earnings. The guarantee of income on participation capital is limited to 24 per cent, the latter for the entire duration of the guarantee. This guarantee covers investment risks up to a maximum of 70 per cent of the sum invested. The guarantee for equity capital is reduced by at least 5 per cent per annum of the initial capital guaranteed. The premium for coverage against non–commercial risks is 1.25 per cent per annum of the current amount. The same percentage is applicable to loan capital for coverage against transfer risk and insolvency or refusal to pay, while for income on capital it is equal to 4 per cent of the anticipated annual income. For investments involving particularly large risks, the premium can be doubled. If certain risks are absent the rate can be reduced by an appropriate amount. If the government of the host country does not guarantee the repayment of funds to the foreign investor, the premium is increased by 0.5 per cent of the amount of loan capital.

Fiscal Measures

There are no special tax advantages in Switzerland to promote direct investment in developing countries. The Confederation and the Cantons have formal agreements for the avoidance of double taxation of income with the following developing countries: South Korea, Malaysia, Pakistan, Singapore, Sri Lanka, Trinidad and Tobago.

P. United Kingdom

Bilateral Investment Protection Agreements

It is the Government's declared policy to conclude as many international protection of property agreements (IPPA) as possible to stimulate investment flows bilaterally. The United Kingdom has traditionally been a major investor overseas and, in terms of book value, is the world's second largest investor. To date, the United Kingdom has signed 30 bilateral IPPAs, the majority with developing countries, 25 of which are in force. The Government is currently negotiating further agreements with countries in Latin America, Africa and the Caribbean.

Investment Guarantee Scheme

The scheme, which came into operation in July 1972, is administered by the Export Credits Guarantee Department, ECGD[26] and applies to new investments in virtually all foreign countries. In principle, all companies carrying on business in the United Kingdom, or companies controlled by them, are eligible for a guarantee, except unincorporated branches of foreign companies and their subsidiaries used solely for channelling investment funds.

To be eligible, the investment must be regarded as assisting the development of the host country, and must be approved by that country. Cover is in principle available for eligible investment in any legally constituted foreign enterprise — including an unincorporated branch of the investor or a partnership — carrying on business in any country outside the United Kingdom.

The scheme provides coverage for equity and loan investments against the three principal categories of political risk (i.e., expropriation, war and restriction on remittances) and is primarily intended to cover those investments in which the investor has a management or trading interest. Cover is also available for portfolio investment, provided that it represents at least 20 per cent of the total capital of the project and is not less than £50 000. As the scheme is designed to encourage lasting investment, the investor must intend to maintain his equity investment for at least three years, whereas eligible loans must have a mean repayment period of not less than three years.

The maximum period of coverage is fifteen years. Coverage can be given for the initial investment and for remitted and retained earnings, but in total not normally exceeding 300 per cent of the initial investment. In the event of loss, the payable claim will not exceed 90 per cent of the amount covered. Premium rates vary between 0.7 per cent and 1 per cent per annum of the amount currently at risk, plus a commitment premium of one–quarter of the country rate on any additional amount which ECGD is committed to insure in future years.

ECGD is able to assume liabilities of up to £750 million ($1.2 billion). Total liabilities outstanding at the end of 1986 were $180 million.

Fiscal Measures

In general, the United Kingdom domestic fiscal system does not have any measure designed specifically to favour direct investment in developing countries. But the United Kingdom has comprehensive double taxation agreements with 77 countries (including most of the Commonwealth), and usually gives unilateral relief for taxes levied by non–agreement countries. Some of these agreements contain "matching credit" provisions, which prevent industrial tax relief by developing countries from being undermined by corresponding increases in the United Kingdom.

A United Kingdom resident investing in an overseas company is generally liable to taxes on the gross amount of the foreign dividend, but credit is given for any foreign withholding tax. Moreover, where the United Kingdom investor is a corporation owning 10 per cent of the foreign company, relief is also given for the foreign tax charged on the profits out of which the dividend is paid. Where the foreign tax exceeds the United Kingdom tax on the dividend, the excess is not allowed as relief against other profits. The situation for overseas branches is similar: the foreign tax on the branch profits can be used as a credit against the United Kingdom tax on the same profits.

Under the imputation system of corporation tax introduced in 1973, a company resident in the United Kingdom pays corporation tax at a single rate, at present 35 per cent full rate or 27 per cent rate for small companies (with profits less than £100 000). All profits, whether distributed or not, are taxable. When the company pays a dividend, it makes an advance payment of corporation tax (ACT), at present calculated at 27 per cent of the amount of the dividend, which, subject to some restriction, it can set against its ultimate corporation tax liability. A United Kingdom resident shareholder receives a tax credit equal to the amount of ACT accounted for by the company in respect of its dividend. This tax credit satisfies its liability to basic rate income tax, so if it is only liable to tax at that rate, it does not pay tax on the dividend. If it is liable at a higher rate it pays the amount by which tax at that rate exceeds the tax credit. But if it is not liable to income tax it is able to reclaim the tax credit.

The Commonwealth Development Corporation, CDC

The Commonwealth Development Corporation (CDC)[27], set up in 1948, is the longest–established development corporation of its type. While responsible to the Overseas Development Administration, CDC has a considerable degree of autonomy as a statutory corporation. The Secretary of State for Foreign and Commonwealth Affairs appoints the Chairman and Members of the Board, which is responsible for CDC staff.

CDC currently aims to make not less than 60 per cent of its new commitments in poorer developing countries and 40 per cent in renewable natural resources projects. CDC invests in ventures implemented and managed by others, as well as in ventures which are developed, controlled and managed by itself. Investments take the form of equity participation, debentures and loans, including loans to governments and statutory bodies. CDC particularly favours joint ventures with local entrepreneurs and local capital. It attaches great importance to sound management and is prepared to provide direct project management, as well as technical support services where requested. Its investments may be made in any developing country, subject to the Secretary of State's approval. CDC invests in a wide range of activities in both the public and private sectors, and tends to concentrate on countries where the private capital sector is relatively weak. Except for economic infrastructure, the emphasis is on large agricultural and medium–sized industrial projects. In the latter field CDC has helped to establish a number of local development finance companies to reach the smaller projects.

CDC has considerable investments in the renewable natural resources sector — agriculture, ranching and forestry — together with allied processing plants (50 per cent of total commitments). Technical, managerial, and financial assistance is given to plantations and small–holder schemes growing bananas, cocoa, sugar cane, rubber, palm oil, tea and tobacco. Over the years CDC has developed an original technique of assisting family small–holders through the establishment of "nucleus estates". These estates operate on commercial lines and encourage the settlement of out–growers. Such estates can provide credit and technical assistance to farmers, process their crops and, ultimately, become the property of the small–holders through the purchase of CDC's shares. CDC is also heavily engaged in basic infrastructure (25 per cent), principally medium–sized investments in power and water. Housing finance (both mortgage financing institutions and housing estate development corporations) and development finance (where CDC investment is usually in association with local governments) each account for 5 per cent of total commitments. CDC also has commitments in industrial plants such as cement, textiles, and chemicals (10 per cent), minerals production (1 per cent), and transport and hotels (1 per cent). As to the geographic distribution of CDC's activities, out of total commitments of £972 million, 45 per cent have been made in Africa, 28 per cent in Asia, 11 per cent in the Pacific Islands, 9 per cent in Latin America and 7 per cent in the Caribbean.

When a project has been successfully established, CDC may dispose of its investments to local or international investors. CDC has no share capital and operates on funds borrowed from the British aid programme and other sources, and on earnings from its investments. Advances from the aid programme to CDC are made at fixed rates of interest below current market rates. Under the current legislation CDC's borrowing limit is £750 million, of which up to £700 million may be borrowed from the aid programme. At the end of December 1986, CDC's approved capital commitments totalled £972 million ($1.6 billion).

Other Official Support

Official Development Assistance funds can be used to finance infrastructure for investment projects. ODA also provides local development institutions with funds for joint ventures involving private investment with local investors or public bodies of the host country. Support is available on a government–to–government basis and a request is needed from the host country before the aid funds can be allocated.

Under the official technical assistance programme the services of experts and consultants can be requested by host countries for drawing up development plans which may include a role for overseas private investment. In co–operation with the Overseas Development Administration, United Kingdom industry provides many courses for trainees from developing countries.

Q. United States

Exchange Control

Outward direct investment by United States residents is free.

Bilateral Investment Protection Agreements

The purpose of the US Bilateral Investment Treaty (BIT) programme, which was initiated in 1981, is to encourage investments in developing countries by guaranteeing US investors a stable and equitable legal framework for their investments. The BITs provide for a) the better of most–favoured–nation or national treatment; b) international law standards for expropriation and compensation; c) unrestricted financial transfers; and d) mechanisms for settlement of investment disputes. BITs are negotiated by the Office of the United States Trade Representative, working with the Department of State and other US government agencies.

The United States has signed ten BITs. The countries are: Bangladesh, Cameroon, Egypt, Grenada, Haiti, Morocco, Panama, Senegal, Turkey and Zaire. Of these, eight have received Senate advice and consent to ratification and were ratified by the President on 6th December 1988.

Investment Guarantee Programmes

The United States has placed a renewed stress on increasing the flow of investment to developing countries. Although the US government does not generally provide special incentives for direct private investment in developing countries, many US government agencies and programmes do encourage and facilitate US direct private investment in developing countries as a component or by–product of their general activities. The United States believes that investment flows should follow market forces and that the best way for developing countries to attract additional foreign direct private investment is to improve their domestic investment climates.

Overseas Private Investment Corporation (OPIC)

The US Congress established the Overseas Private Investment Corporation[28] as an independent entity in 1971 to encourage US private investment in developing countries. OPIC inherited a wide variety of private investment activities from the US Agency for International Development (US AID). It groups in one institution a range of programmes that in other countries are normally divided between an investment guaranty agency and a development finance agency. OPIC conducts its finance and insurance operations on a self–sustaining basis, taking into account sound underwriting and portfolio management as well as the economic and financial viability of individual projects.

OPIC supports only those projects that contribute to the economic and social development of the host country and are consistent with US balance–of–payments and employment objectives. In addition, OPIC will not support projects subject to performance requirements that would reduce substantially the positive trade benefits likely to accrue to the United States from the investment. In its 1985 extension of OPIC's operating authority, the US Congress prohibited OPIC from assisting any projects that a) would pose an unreasonable environmental, health, or safety hazard, or would degrade national parks or protected areas, or b) are in countries that have not taken steps to adopt and implement laws extending internationally recognised workers' rights. The 1988 legislation that reauthorised OPIC programmes for an additional four years also included a number of initiatives designed to enhance OPIC's development mandate. These included a) a $10 million equity programme that enables OPIC to make equity investments in projects in Sub–Saharan Africa and the Caribbean, and b) authority to finance the development of new technologies by small businesses in the United States to enhance economic and social development in less developed countries.

OPIC gives preferential treatment to investments in LDCs with per capita incomes of less than $984 (1986 US dollars), and restricts its activities in developing countries with per capita incomes greater than $2 600 (1986 US dollars). As of 30th April 1989, OPIC is authorised to operate in 109 countries.

OPIC is governed by a 15–member board of directors, composed of eight members from the private sector and seven from the US government. The Chairman is the Administrator of the Agency for International Development (AID), ex officio, and the Vice–Chairman is a Deputy US Trade Representative. The five other public sector directors represent the Departments of State, Treasury, Commerce, and Labour, and OPIC itself. The President of the United States, with the advice and consent of the US Senate, appoints the eight private sector directors and the president of OPIC.

a) Investment Insurance Programme

Insurance against the political risk of currency inconvertibility was introduced in 1948 as part of the Marshall Plan. Since then, the programme has expanded to include insurance coverage against loss of investment caused by expropriation and political violence and, most recently, to include losses from business interruption due to political violence.

The Investment Insurance Programme, formerly known as the Specific Risk Guaranty Programme, offers a variety of investors protection against loss due to three broad political risk categories: a) currency inconvertibility, b) expropriation, and c) political violence (war, revolution, insurrection, and civil strife).

Besides insuring typical equity, debt, and guaranty instruments, OPIC also offers coverage against arbitrary drawdowns of standby letters of credit issued as bid, advance payment, and performance guarantees on behalf of US contractors and exporters. OPIC insures US construction firms against disputes, in addition to the political risks listed above. OPIC has developed comprehensive insurance coverage for investments in oil and gas exploration, development and production, including production–sharing agreements, service contracts, risk contracts, and traditional concessions. OPIC also provides insurance for US investors involved in international and cross–border leasing.

Coverage is issued for a maximum of twenty years. OPIC insures up to 90 per cent of an investment and its associated earnings, except for investments by institutional investors, for whom OPIC will insure 100 per cent. Fees are based on the apparent risk of each project, and average about 0.3 per cent for inconvertibility coverage and 0.6 per cent for each of expropriation and political violence. Eligible investments can be made in the form of cash, materials and equipment, technology, or services. OPIC will only insure new investments or expansions of existing investment made by investors meeting certain US citizenship criteria. All projects must be approved by the host government.

As of 31st December 1988, OPIC's maximum potential liability under its Investment Insurance Programme was approximately $3.1 billion. Since its inception, OPIC has endeavored to keep its risks within manageable limits, including limiting its exposure in any one country to 10 per cent of its worldwide exposure.

b) *Project Finance Programme*

The Investment Loan Guaranty Programme, formerly known as the Extended Risk Guaranty Programme, provides non–recourse medium to long–term dollar financing in selected countries. OPIC can guarantee loans covering up to 50 per cent of the cost of a new project and 75 per cent of the cost of an expansion. Any number of US financial institutions are eligible to fund OPIC guarantees. These include commercial and investment banks, insurance companies, and pension funds. Generally, OPIC requires US management participation, and a reasonable financial stake in the enterprise.

Because the guaranty, which covers both commercial as well as political risks, is backed by the "full faith and credit" of the US government, the interest rate on the underlying loan reflects US government agency rates and not the credit of the borrower. A guaranty fee is charged on outstanding loan balances, which varies according to the project's political and financial risk, and averages about 2 per cent per year. The loan can be at either a fixed or a floating rate, typically tied to the rates of US Treasury obligations. There are also facility and commitment fees. The former, a one–time up–front fee, averages 1 per cent, and the latter 2/3 per cent on undrawn balances. Investment guaranties can range from $2 million to $25 million.

The US Congress annually determines the amount of loans that OPIC can guarantee, which is currently $175 million. As of 31st December 1988, $405.7 million of guaranties were outstanding.

Another important OPIC programme is the Direct Investment Fund, which was established in 1969 to provide loans to projects for which private financing on appropriate terms is unavailable. Direct loans are available only to US small businesses or co-operatives. Interest rates are fixed, and they approximate long-term fixed rates in commercial money markets. There are also facility and commitment fees. These loans generally range from $500 000 to $6 million. Like the guaranty programme, the US Congress also determines the amount that OPIC an directly lend, currently set at $23 million. The Fund's portfolio was $52 million as of 31st December 1988.

OPIC also has equity and equity participating instruments. In addition to providing debt capital, OPIC can provide permanent capital through capital stock investments and the purchase of a project's debentures convertible to stock. In these cases, owners share their equity in a project with OPIC. This permits them to reduce their exposure to risk and, by improving the project's capital base, often makes it possible to obtain substantially more debt capital for the project as well. OPIC does not seek to acquire a majority stake in any company, participate in its day-to-day management, or remain an investor beyond the first few years of operations. An OPIC investment will generally be in the $250 000 to $2 million range, but in exceptional circumstances could be higher. Currently, OPIC will consider an investment in the common or preferred stock of companies only in certain geographic regions — 40 countries in Sub-Saharan Africa and 20 in Central America and the Caribbean. Although projects sponsored by US companies of any size are eligible, OPIC will give preferential consideration to projects significantly involving US small businesses or co-operatives.

c) *Investment Encouragement Activities*

To further foster private investment in developing countries, OPIC offers several investment encouragement services. These include the Investment Missions Programme, the Opportunity Bank, and an Investor Information Service. OPIC conducts investment missions to developing countries four or five times a year, during which US business executives meet host-country business leaders, government officials, and potential joint-venture partners. OPIC organised investment missions to 31 developing countries between 1981 and 30th September 1988, resulting in over $464 million of new investments.

OPIC's Opportunity Bank is a computerised data base that matches US companies with investment projects in developing countries. Currently, the Opportunity Bank contains profiles of more than 2 000 investment projects in 95 developing countries, and a listing of over 1 800 potential US investors.

OPIC created the Investor Information Service to assist US investors in gathering basic information about developing countries and their business environments. The Investor Information Service provides investor kits containing information from a variety of US government agencies and international organisations. Investor kits are available for more than 110 developing countries and 16 regions. Each kit provides information on the country's or region's economy, trade laws, business practices, political conditions, and investment incentives.

The US Agency for International Development (AID)

AID relies upon a variety of mechanisms to promote foreign direct investment and to address the financial markets problems in developing countries. AID programmes are administered by missions in over 70 countries, many of which have private sector officers. These officers are available to assist the US business community to secure available information and assistance regarding business investment in a particular country or region. Similar information is provided from private sector offices in AID's Washington, DC headquarters. AID also has been able to help formulate US government policy on international investment issues through its participation in the US government's investment policy co–ordination process.

a) *Policy Reform and Technical Assistance*

Policy dialogue, conditioned assistance, and related technical assistance to influence change in host–government policies are essential elements of AID's programme to promote foreign investment and to help developing countries make their economies more attractive to potential private foreign and local investors.

Policy reforms are also sought in related areas such as *a)* import regimes, where AID seeks the freeing of exchange rates, eliminating access restrictions on foreign exchange, and reducing restrictive licensing and prohibitive tariffs, and *b)* exchange controls, where AID has contributed to the reduction of economic controls and minimised the effect of these market distortions upon savings and investment.

b) *Project–related Assistance to Promote FDI*

Many AID private sector projects are designed to encourage *a)* greater awareness of trade and investment opportunities by the US and developing–country business communities, *b)* full understanding by both US and developing–country business communities of the incentives offered by certain US legislation, and *c)* increased private sector investment.

AID assists developing countries in the establishment of investment promotion agencies. The major purposes of these agencies are to *a)* attract and provide investment services for potential investors, including streamlined or one–stop investment approval centres, and *b)* influence host–country policy–makers on the changes needed to reform investment policies, regulations, and processes. Through direct targeting of US companies (via investment promotion offices in the United States) and other mechanisms, these agencies have helped to create thousands of new jobs and generate millions of dollars of investment in many developing countries.

AID also supports the establishment of free trade zones and some infrastructure development in developing countries. AID helps to upgrade the infrastructure needed to attract private investment, such as road or irrigation improvement projects.

AID programmes in privatisation and debt/equity swaps offer opportunities for foreign investment. In some instances, divested state enterprises are being purchased by foreign concerns that invest new resources and technologies into these former state enterprises. Debt–equity conversion programmes contribute to economic growth through the promotion of policy reforms that support growth and investment.

c) *Assistance to Improve Developing–Country Financial Markets*

AID's efforts to promote financial markets development are also important for promoting investment. AID has been active in helping developing countries improve their financial systems through technical assistance, training, and the provision of credit. AID supports policy reforms and incentives meant to restore domestic business confidence, rationalise interest rates, and attract foreign investment.

Two policy areas critical to encouraging foreign direct investment and promoting increased local investment are the removal of interest rate controls and tax policy reform. AID has been instrumental in bringing about market–determined interest rates and in reducing reliance upon artificial allocations of credit, which have the effect of attracting foreign investment and discouraging capital flight. AID has also made tax reform an integral part of its policy dialogue with developing countries, contributing to a reduction of marginal tax rates and the removal of disincentives to productive investment in many countries.

The investment programme managed by AID's Bureau for Private Enterprise is developing new investment concepts, instruments, and approaches for mobilisation of investment capital within developing–country and international financial markets. Among the innovative financial mechanisms being experimented with to stimulate foreign investment and indigenous private sector development are mobilising international sources of private sector venture capital; taking advantage of blocked funds, debt–to–equity conversion programmes and other capital leveraging methods; and marshalling innovative credit enhancement strategies such as securitisation.

Fiscal Measures

The United States taxes the worldwide income of its corporations, citizens, and residents. To avoid double taxation, the United States allows a credit for income taxes paid to foreign governments. This credit, however, is limited to the taxes that would have been paid to the US Treasury if the income had been earned domestically. Moreover, the limitation is computed by the "overall" method; that is, by adding all foreign taxes and income. Since this method allows taxes from high and low tax countries to be averaged, income from low tax countries that would be subject to US tax under a "per country" method may not be subject to US tax under the "overall" method. The 1986 Tax Reform Act created a large number of "baskets" for particularly high or low taxed income. Since limitations must be computed separately for these baskets, the avoidance of US tax by means of averaging should be mitigated.

US tax laws offer no special incentives for investment in developing countries as opposed to developed countries. Nevertheless, certain features of US or foreign tax systems may encourage investment abroad. First, the US does not tax income of controlled foreign corporations that is not repatriated to the United States; however, if an overseas entity is organised as a branch rather than a controlled foreign corporation, all income is subject to tax. It is sometimes argued that this feature, referred to as deferral, encourages investment abroad. Subpart F rules tend to mitigate any effect that deferral might have by subjecting passive investment income to tax currently. The 1986 Tax Reform Act strengthened Subpart F rules. Second, certain countries (but not the United States) grant "tax holidays". That is, some countries exempt or greatly lower the tax of foreign corporations for a period of time. Third, tax holidays are sometimes accompanied by "tax sparing", under which the home country grants credit for taxes that would have been paid had the tax holiday not existed. The United States does not engage in tax sparing. Fourth, the United States negotiates bilateral tax treaties that are useful for both countries in exchanging taxpayer information and reducing "withholding taxes" that are often placed on gross income flows and therefore can have very high effective rates.

Other Official Support

The US Export–Import Bank (Ex–Im), an independent agency of the US government, facilitates US exports by providing loans, guarantees, and insurance to foreign buyers and US manufacturers. Ex–Im's export credit activities are associated with increased US foreign investment.

The United States signed the Convention establishing the Multilateral Investment Guarantee Agency (MIGA), the newest part of the World Bank group. MIGA is designed to promote private sector development in developing countries by offering investment insurance and encouraging policy reform.

The United States Congress enacted the Caribbean Basin Recovery Act (CBRA) in 1983. This act, which formed the basis of the Caribbean Basin Initiative (CBI), provided designated Caribbean Basin countries with twelve years of US duty–free treatment of most export products. In 1986, CBRA was strengthened to permit CBI countries with Tax Information Exchange Agreements to finance new investment with funds generated in Puerto Rico and loaned at favourable terms.

4. MULTILATERAL PROGRAMMES

This section describes a number of multilateral and international schemes and initiatives which are not sponsored by any one DAC Member country in particular, but in which DAC Member governments or firms participate. The various institutions are designed to provide incentives or protection for overseas private investment from developed countries. Schemes of a public nature are sponsored by public multilateral institutions (United Nations, World Bank, etc.). The institutions discussed are not intended to substitute for national schemes of incentives but rather to complement them and, in some cases, to provide machinery for co–operation between them.

a) European Economic Community

The first Lomé Convention was succeeded by Lomé II (1980) and Lomé III (1985). Negotiations are now at an advanced stage for a Fourth Lomé Convention. Lomé III, the present Convention, covers both trade arrangements and development assistance.

Industrial co–operation activities are entrusted to the Commission of the European Communities, the European Investment Bank (EIB), and the Centre for the Development of Industry.

The Commission of the European Communities manages the resources of the European Development Fund (EDF) in the form of subsidies and special loans. The EDF subsidises special low–interest rates on loans given by the EIB, which is also in charge of managing the EDF's risk capital. The Sixth European Development Fund, (EDF VI) covered by the Third Lomé Convention, includes the following amounts:

4 880 million ECU for grants
600 million ECU for special loans
600 million ECU for risk capital

Amongst the Convention's many provisions, Articles 60–74 deal specifically with industrial development. Article 65 of the Convention States, inter–alia, that particular attention shall be paid to:

— Industries for the domestic processing of raw materials;
— Agro–industries;
— Integral industries capable of creating links between the different sectors of the economy;
— Industries which have a favourable effect on employment, the trade balance and regional integration.

The Convention stipulates that, as a matter of priority, Community financing is to take the form of loans from the European Investment Bank, on its resources, and of risk capital, these being the specific financing methods for industrial enterprises. In addition to these activities, other articles provide for the following:

— Improvement of the institutional framework of ACP countries;
— Reinforcement of the ACP countries' financial institutions;
— Creation, rehabilitation, and improvement of infrastructures for industry;
— Integration of industrial structures and regional or inter–regional markets;
— Development of ACP–EEC and intra–ACP co–operation between enterprises by means of information and industrial promotion activities (in which the Centre for the Development of Industry — a joint ACP–EEC body — is accorded a significant role);
— Activities to facilitate the development of small and medium–sized enterprises;
— Activities to improve the technologies available to ACP industries;
— Assistance for the training of ACP nationals.

Finance for development assistance in respect of these operations in ACP countries is provided from the European Investment Bank. This takes the form of loans from its own resources and of risk capital made available under the Convention, and from the Sixth European Development Fund.

The European Investment Bank is in charge of financing, in a general way, projects and programmes for productive activities. Sectors include industry, agro–industry, tourism, mining, energy production, transport and telecommunications. (The priority sectors do not rule out the possibility of the Bank's financing other programmes in productive activities). For Lomé III the EIB is in charge of 1 100 ECU own–resource funds, and of 600 million ECU risk capital at the Commission's disposal.

Interest rates and repayment periods are set according to the particular characteristics of each project, but at present, the average interest rate applied to loans on own–resources is 5 per cent and for loans on risk capital 2 per cent. Repayment periods range from about 15 years for loans on own–resources to about 25 years for loans on risk–capital.

Most loans granted by the Bank exceed 1 million ECU. In the case of small and medium–sized enterprises whose financing needs are less than this, the Bank's current practice is to intervene through global loans, development banks or other financial institutions in ACP countries.

Special loans have a 40–year repayment period with a 10–year grace period, and carry a 1 per cent interest rate. Loans to the very least developed countries carry an interest rate of 0.5 per cent.

b) International Centre for Settlement of Investment Disputes, ICSID

One of the principal purposes of the "Convention on the Settlement of Investment Disputes between States and Nationals of Other States" was the creation of a mechanism for settling disputes involving a government on the one side and a foreign private investor on the other. The ICSID was thus established under the auspices of the World Bank to encourage the growth of private foreign investment by creating the possibility of settling such disputes by conciliation or arbitration.

The Convention specifies the circumstances and methods under which disputes may be submitted to the Centre and the form and effects of the resulting conciliation or arbitration proceedings. A growing number of investment agreements include provisions to submit future disputes to the Centre and a number of host countries have adopted legislation to accept the Centre's jurisdiction.

The governing body of the Centre is its administrative council. It is composed of one representative of each contracting state, normally the governor appointed by the states to the World Bank, unless a specific designation is made. Its seat is established at the IBRD headquarters. As of April 1989, the Convention on the Settlement of Investment Disputes had been signed by 97 States, 91 of which had completed ratification. Membership is heaviest in Africa, while few South American countries have joined. All industrialised Member countries of the OECD except Canada are members of the ICSID (Australia being the only Member which has not yet ratified the Convention).

Since the jurisdiction of the Centre is based on consent, the most likely cases to come before the Centre are disputes arising out of contractual arrangements which include an ICSID arbitration or conciliation clause. The Convention permits submission of existing disputes in the absence of a previous ICSID arbitration or conciliation clause. Such disputes will normally have arisen in the context of relationships which date back to pre–Convention days. In the absence of an obligation to come to the Centre, the host states generally prefer to seek a settlement with the home state of the investor. As of 30th June 1987, 23 disputes had been submitted to ICSID. The fact that there are not more cases before the Centre is not considered as an indication that the Convention is not serving a useful purpose, because the inclusion of an effective arbitration clause in new investment arrangements may result in an actual reduction in the number of disputes.

The Centre has published a survey entitled *Investment Laws of the World*, which deals with national law and international agreements affecting foreign investment in developing countries on a country–by–country basis. It compiles constitutional, legislative, regulatory and treaty materials. Its objectives are to assist states in comparing investment promotion instruments in various parts of the world and to familiarise potential investors with legal conditions in various countries. Since 1986, the Centre has also published the ICSID Review, *Foreign Investment Law Journal*.

c) The International Chamber of Commerce, ICC

In 1923 the ICC set up the International Court of Arbitration, which plays a very active role in the settlement of investment disputes. The ICC Court of Arbitration can settle disputes between a foreign investor and the host–country government, or between the investor and parties that are nationals of or established in the host country. Parties must adhere to the 1958 New York Convention on the recognition and enforcement of foreign arbitral awards. Parties must also have included in their contracts an arbitration clause referring to the International Court of Arbitration.

d) Multilateral Investment Guarantee Agency, MIGA

Since national guarantee systems often fail to meet investors needs, a proposal to establish a multilateral facility for guaranteeing international investment has been periodically discussed since the early 1960s. One regional agency, the Inter–Arab Investment Guarantee Agency, was established in 1974, but its operations are limited to investments by nationals of the Arab member countries. More recently, a plan to create the Multilateral Investment Guarantee Agency (MIGA) under the auspices of the World Bank has come to fruition. The MIGA is an autonomous agency financed through subscriptions from developed and developing countries. It commenced operations in June 1988. As of April 1989, 39 developing countries and 12 OECD countries had ratified the convention, and an additional 22 had signed but not yet ratified the agreement.

MIGA's purpose is to promote the flow of FDI to Member developing countries *a)* by issuing guarantees (including co–insurance with, and re–insurance of, existing political risk insurers) against non–commercial risks, and *b)* by providing various advisory and technical services to assist member developing countries' efforts to attract foreign investment.

MIGA will only insure projects which are of clear developmental benefit to the host country and are not dependent upon subsidies. MIGA will insure both conventional direct and portfolio investments and contractual forms of investment such as management and technical arrangements in which the foreign contractor's remuneration is substantially dependent upon the performance of the assisted enterprise. Production and profit–sharing contracts, franchises, licences, leasing, and turnkey contracts are examples of such forms of contracted investment. The range of risks covered by MIGA will be extended to include (in addition to war, civil unrest, riots and terrorism, and expropriation) "creeping expropriation", defined as a series of host–country measures whose combined effect is expropriatory. Coverage of currency inconvertibility will include transfer risk. MIGA will also, under certain conditions, provide insurance against breach of contract.

In addition to its insurance activities, MIGA will supplement the activities of the World Bank and IFC in promoting investments by carrying out research, providing information, rendering technical assistance and fostering consultations among managers of investment–promotion agencies of some countries. MIGA may become instrumental in inducing the return of flight capital, as residents of developing countries may obtain its insurance with their governments' consent if they invest their flight capital in their home countries. MIGA may also become a catalyst for the conversion of bank debt into equity, as coverage may be extended to this category of investment.

Initially, MIGA will be able to cover some $1.5 billion of investments (with no country risk exceeding 5 per cent of the total). The convention allows MIGA to increase its underwriting ceiling to five times subscriptions, that is to a cumulative total of some $5 billion.

MIGA would be subrogated to the rights of indemnified investors against host countries. Disputes between the agency and host countries are to be settled by negotiation and ultimately may be submitted to international arbitration. A host country's sovereignty is safeguarded by the principle that both the investments and the agency's guarantee must be approved by its authorities.

e) Guarantees by Private Insurers

Some commercial insurers insure investors against foreign political risks. Both existing and new investments can be insured, regardless of whether they are eligible for official guarantees.

Private insurance may be sought by an individual or a corporation for any asset held abroad, whether it consists of participation in subsidiaries, assets held in outright ownership, loans or other rights. This insurance is based on the declared value of the assets to be insured — in principle their real value — as opposed to the transferred amount, as is the case with official guarantees.

The duration of the guarantee contract is usually one year. It is renewable, but not automatically. In this event there may be a revaluation of the amount insured. The proportion covered is normally 90 per cent, but may be as high as 100 per cent. The premium depends mainly on the country concerned, but also on the nature of the investment and the geographical spread of coverage given to a single insured party. Even though premiums for private contracts are generally much higher than for official contracts (between 1 and 5 per cent, depending on the type of investment, country, duration, etc.), private political risk insurance might be relatively cheap. In such cases companies are not obliged to accept the whole "package" (as is normally the case with public bodies, which insure the whole value of the investment), but only the portion that the investor believes to be especially vulnerable to political risk. In this way premiums can be kept down.

Guarantees cover loss or damage which result directly from the following acts: confiscation, expropriation, nationalisation, seizure, appropriation, requisition, deliberate destruction of assets or of their title of ownership, or any other act amounting to deprivation resulting in total cessation of business.

NOTES AND REFERENCES

1. AUSTRADE-EFIC, P.O. Box R65, Royal Exchange, NSW 2000, Australia, Telephone (61 2) 561-0111, Telex EFIC AA 121224, Telefax (61 2) 251-3851.

2. OKB, Am Hof 4, P.O. Box 70, A-1011 Vienna, Austria, Telephone 53 12 70, Telex 13-27 85, Telefax 53127/693, Cable: Kontrollbank Wien.

3. OND, Square de Meeûs 40, 1040 Brussels, Belgium.

4. AGCD, Building "A.G.", Place du Champ de Mars 5 Bte 57, 1050 Brussels, Belgium, Telex 21-376, 22162, 22165, 22166, BELEXT.

5. Through a provisional fund, Belgium has already acquired a stake in the Banque Rwandaises de Développement, the Banque Nationale de Développement Economique du Burundi and the (sub-regional) Banque de Développement des Etats des Grands Lacs (BDEGL).

6. SBI, 63 rue Montoyer B-1040 Brussels, Belgium, Telephone (02) 230-27-85; telegraphic address: Investbel, Bruxelles; Telex 25744, SNIM, attention SBI.

7. EDC, 151 O'Connor Street, P.O. Box 655, Ottawa, Ontario K1P 5T9, Canada, Telephone (613) 598-2500, Telex 053-4136, Cable: EXCREDCORP.

8. Danida, 2 Asiatisk Plads, DK-1448 Copenhagen K., Denmark, Telephone 01-92 00 00, Telex 31292 etr DK.

9. IFU, 4, Bremerholm, DK-1069 Copenhagen K., Denmark, Telephone +45-142575, Fax +45-1-322524, Telex 15493 DK.

10. VTL, Etelaranta 6, P.O. Box 187, SF-00131 Helsinki 13, Finland, Telephone 661-811, Telex 121778 vtl sf.

11. FINNFUND, Ratakatu 27, P.O. Box 391, SF-00121 Helsinki, Finland, Telephone (+358 0) 641301, Telex 125028 fund SF. Telefax (+358 0) 603309.

12. Banque Francaise du Commerce Extérieur, 21, Boulevard Haussmann, 75009 Paris, France, Telephone: 42 47 47 47, Telex: 660370.

13. Compagnie Francaise d'Assurance pour le Commerce Extérieur, 12, cours Michelet, La Defense 10, 92800 Puteaux, France, Telephone 49 02 20 00, Telex 614884.

14. CCCE, Cité Retiro, 35-37, rue Boissy d'Anglas, 75379 Paris Cedex 08, France, Telephone 40 06 31 31, Telex 212632.

15. Treuarbeit AG, New York Ring 13, D-2000 Hamburg 60, Federal Republic of Germany, Telephone (49-40) 6378-1, Telex tahh d 2174118.

16. Deutsche Finanzierungsgesellschaft für Beteiligungen in Entwicklungslandern, GmbH. (DEG), Belvedere-Strasse 40, D-5000 Köln 41, Federal Republic of Germany, Telephone (221) 49861, Telex 8881949; Cable deutschges koeln.

17. Bundesstelle für Aussenhandelsinformation, Am Blaubach 13, D-5000 Köln, Federal Republic of Germany, Telephone (49-221) 2057-1.

18. MITI, 1-3-1, Kasumigaseki, Chiyoda-Ku, Tokyo 100, Japan, Telephone 81 3 501-1511, Telefax 81 3 501-2081.

19. Eximbank of Japan, 1-4-1 Ohtemachi 1-Chome, Chiyoda-Ku, Tokyo 100, Japan, Telephone 81 3 287-1221.

20. OECF, Takebashi: Godo Bldg. Ohtemachi, 1-Chome, Chiyoda-Ku, Tokyo 100, Japan, Telephone 215.1311, Cable COOPERATIONFUND, Telex J 28790 or J 28430.

21. JICA, Shinjuku Mitsui Bldg. 2-1-1, Nishi-Shinjuku, Shinjuku-Ku, Tokyo 100, Japan, Telephone 03.346.5311, Telex J 22271.

22. NCM, Keizersgracht 271-277, 1016 ED Amsterdam, The Netherlands, Telephone (020) 3202911; Telex 11496 NCM NL

23. FMO, Bezuidenhoutseweg 62, P.O. Box 93060, 2509 AB The Hague, The Netherlands, Telephone (033) (0)70-419641, Fax 033 (0)70 47 17 33, Telex 33042 nefmo nl.

24. EXGO, State Insurance Building, Box 5037, Wellington, New Zealand, Telephone 720265, Telex 31239 STATINS.

25. SWEDFUND, Jacobs Torg 3, S-10327 Stockholm, Box 16360, Sweden, Telephone 08-231 740, Telex 14135 Swefund S.

26. ECGD, Export House, P.O. Box 272, London EC4M 7AY, United Kingdom, Telephone 01-382 7000, Telex 883601.

27. CDC, 33 Hill Street, London W1A 3AR, United Kingdom, Telephone 01-629 8484, Telex 21431.

28. OPIC, 1615 M Street NW, Washington, DC. 20527, United States, Telephone 202-457-7200.

WHERE TO OBTAIN OECD PUBLICATIONS
OÙ OBTENIR LES PUBLICATIONS DE L'OCDE

Argentina – Argentine
Carlos Hirsch S.R.L.
Galería Güemes, Florida 165, 4° Piso
1333 Buenos Aires
    Tel. 30.7122, 331.1787 y 331.2391
Telegram: Hirsch–Baires
Telex: 21112 UAPE–AR. Ref. s/2901
Telefax:(1)331–1787

Australia – Australie
D.A. Book (Aust.) Pty. Ltd.
11–13 Station Street (P.O. Box 163)
Mitcham, Vic. 3132   Tel. (03)873.4411
Telex: AA37911 DA BOOK
Telefax: (03)873.5679

Austria – Autriche
OECD Publications and Information Centre
4 Simrockstrasse
5300 Bonn (Germany) Tel. (0228)21.60.45
Telex: 8 86300 Bonn
Telefax: (0228)26.11.04
Gerold & Co.
Graben 31
Wien I   Tel. (0222)533.50.14

Belgium – Belgique
Jean De Lannoy
Avenue du Roi 202
B–1060 Bruxelles
    Tel. (02)538.51.69/538.08.41
Telex: 63220 Telefax: (02)538.08.41

Canada
Renouf Publishing Company Ltd.
1294 Algoma Road
Ottawa, Ont. K1B 3W8 Tel. (613)741.4333
Telex: 053–4783 Telefax: (613)741.5439
Stores:
61 Sparks Street
Ottawa, Ont. K1P 5R1 Tel. (613)238.8985
211 Yonge Street
Toronto, Ont. M5B 1M4 Tel. (416)363.3171
Federal Publications
165 University Avenue
Toronto, ON M5H 3B9 Tel. (416)581.1552
Telefax: (416)581.1743
Les Publications Fédérales
1185 rue de l'Université
Montréal, PQ H3B 1R7 Tel.(514)954–1633
Les Éditions La Liberté Inc.
3020 Chemin Sainte-Foy
Sainte–Foy, P.Q. G1X 3V6
    Tel. (418)658.3763
Telefax: (418)658.3763

Denmark – Danemark
Munksgaard Export and Subscription Service
35, Nørre Søgade, P.O. Box 2148
DK–1016 København K
    Tel. (45 33)12.85.70
Telex: 19431 MUNKS DK
    Telefax: (45 33)12.93.87

Finland – Finlande
Akateeminen Kirjakauppa
Keskuskatu 1, P.O. Box 128
00100 Helsinki   Tel. (358 0)12141
Telex: 125080 Telefax: (358 0)121.4441

France
OECD/OCDE
Mail Orders/Commandes par correspondance:
2 rue André-Pascal
75775 Paris Cedex 16 Tel. (1)45.24.82.00
Bookshop/Librairie:
33, rue Octave-Feuillet
75016 Paris   Tel. (1)45.24.81.67
    (1)45.24.81.81
Telex: 620 160 OCDE
Telefax: (33-1)45.24.85.00
Librairie de l'Université
12a, rue Nazareth
13602 Aix-en-Provence Tel. 42.26.18.08

Germany – Allemagne
OECD Publications and Information Centre
4 Simrockstrasse
5300 Bonn   Tel. (0228)21.60.45
Telex: 8 86300 Bonn
    Telefax: (0228)26.11.04

Greece – Grèce
Librairie Kauffmann
28 rue du Stade
105 64 Athens   Tel. 322.21.60
Telex: 218187 LIKA Gr

Hong Kong
Government Information Services
Publications (Sales) Office
Information Service Department
No. 1 Battery Path
Central   Tel. (5)23.31.91
Telex: 802.61190

Iceland – Islande
Mál Mog Menning
Laugavegi 18, Pósthólf 392
121 Reykjavik   Tel. 15199/24240

India – Inde
Oxford Book and Stationery Co.
Scindia House
New Delhi 110001 Tel. 331.5896/5308
Telex: 31 61990 AM IN
Telefax: (11)332.5993
17 Park Street
Calcutta 700016   Tel. 240832

Indonesia – Indonésie
Pdii-Lipi
P.O. Box 269/JKSMG/88
Jakarta12790   Tel. 583467
Telex: 62 875

Ireland – Irlande
TDC Publishers – Library Suppliers
12 North Frederick Street
Dublin 1   Tel. 744835/749677
Telex: 33530 TDCP EI Telefax : 748416

Italy – Italie
Libreria Commissionaria Sansoni
Via Benedetto Fortini, 120/10
Casella Post. 552
50125 Firenze Tel. (055)645415
Telex: 570466 Telefax: (39.55)641257
Via Bartolini 29
20155 Milano   Tel. 365083
La diffusione delle pubblicazioni OCSE viene
assicurata dalle principali librerie ed anche
da:
Editrice e Libreria Herder
Piazza Montecitorio 120
00186 Roma   Tel. 679.4628
Telex: NATEL I 621427
Libreria Hoepli
Via Hoepli 5
20121 Milano   Tel. 865446
Telex: 31.33.95 Telefax: (39.2)805.2886
Libreria Scientifica
Dott. Lucio de Biasio "Aeiou"
Via Meravigli 16
20123 Milano   Tel. 807679
Telefax: 800175

Japan– Japon
OECD Publications and Information Centre
Landic Akasaka Building
2–3–4 Akasaka, Minato-ku
Tokyo 107   Tel. 586.2016
Telefax: (81.3)584.7929

Korea – Corée
Kyobo Book Centre Co. Ltd.
P.O. Box 1658, Kwang Hwa Moon
Seoul   Tel. (REP)730.78.91
Telefax: 735.0030

Malaysia/Singapore – Malaisie/Singapour
University of Malaya Co-operative Bookshop
Ltd.
P.O. Box 1127, Jalan Pantai Baru 59100
Kuala Lumpur
Malaysia   Tel. 756.5000/756.5425
Telefax: 757.3661
Information Publications Pte. Ltd.
Pei–Fu Industrial Building
24 New Industrial Road No. 02–06
Singapore 1953 Tel. 283.1786/283.1798
Telefax: 284.8875

Netherlands – Pays-Bas
SDU Uitgeverij
Christoffel Plantijnstraat 2
Postbus 20014
2500 EA's-Gravenhage Tel. (070)78.99.11
Voor bestellingen: Tel. (070)78.98.80
Telex: 32486 stdru Telefax: (070)47.63.51

New Zealand –Nouvelle-Zélande
Government Printing Office
Customer Services
P.O. Box 12–411
Freepost 10–050
Thorndon, Wellington
Tel. 0800 733–406 Telefax: 04 499–1733

Norway – Norvège
Narvesen Info Center – NIC
Bertrand Narvesens vei 2
P.O. Box 6125 Etterstad
0602 Oslo 6
    Tel. (02)67.83.10/(02)68.40.20
Telex: 79668 NIC N Telefax: (47 2)68.53.47

Pakistan
Mirza Book Agency
65 Shahrah Quaid-E-Azam
Lahore 3   Tel. 66839
Telex: 44886 UBL PK. Attn: MIRZA BK

Portugal
Livraria Portugal
Rua do Carmo 70–74
1117 Lisboa Codex Tel. 347.49.82/3/4/5

Singapore/Malaysia Singapour/Malaisie
See "Malaysia/Singapore"
Voir "Malaisie/Singapour"

Spain – Espagne
Mundi-Prensa Libros S.A.
Castello 37, Apartado 1223
Madrid 28001   Tel. (91) 431.33.99
Telex: 49370 MPLI Telefax: (91) 275.39.98
Libreria Internacional AEDOS
Consejo de Ciento 391
08009 –Barcelona Tel. (93) 301–86–15
Telefax: (93) 317–01–41

Sweden – Suède
Fritzes Fackboksföretaget
Box 16356, S 103 27 STH
Regeringsgatan 12
DS Stockholm   Tel. (08)23.89.00
Telex: 12387 Telefax: (08)20.50.21
Subscription Agency/Abonnements:
Wennergren–Williams AB
Box 30004
104 25 Stockholm Tel. (08)54.12.00
Telex: 19937 Telefax: (08)50.82.86

Switzerland – Suisse
OECD Publications and Information Centre
4 Simrockstrasse
5300 Bonn (Germany) Tel. (0228)21.60.45
Telex: 8 86300 Bonn
Telefax: (0228)26.11.04
Librairie Payot
6 rue Grenus
1211 Genève 11   Tel. (022)731.89.50
Telex: 28356
Maditec S.A.
Ch. des Palettes 4
1020 Renens/Lausanne Tel. (021)635.08.65
Telefax: (021)635.07.80
United Nations Bookshop/Librairie des Nations-Unies
Palais des Nations
1211 Genève 10
    Tel. (022)734.60.11 (ext. 48.72)
Telex: 289696 (Attn: Sales)
Telefax: (022)733.98.79

Taïwan – Formose
Good Faith Worldwide Int'l. Co. Ltd.
9th Floor, No. 118, Sec. 2
Chung Hsiao E. Road
Taipei   Tel. 391.7396/391.7397
Telefax: (02) 394.9176

Thailand – Thalande
Suksit Siam Co. Ltd.
1715 Rama IV Road, Samyan
Bangkok 5   Tel. 251.1630

Turkey – Turquie
Kültur Yayinlari Is–Türk Ltd. Sti.
Atatürk Bulvari No. 191/Kat. 21
Kavaklidere/Ankara Tel. 25.07.60
Dolmabahce Cad. No. 29
Besiktas/Istanbul Tel. 160.71.88
Telex: 43482B

United Kingdom – Royaume-Uni
H.M. Stationery Office
Gen. enquiries   Tel. (01) 873 0011
Postal orders only:
P.O. Box 276, London SW8 5DT
Personal Callers HMSO Bookshop
49 High Holborn, London WC1V 6HB
Telex: 297138 Telefax: 873.8463
Branches at: Belfast, Birmingham, Bristol,
Edinburgh, Manchester

United States – États-Unis
OECD Publications and Information Centre
2001 L Street N.W., Suite 700
Washington, D.C. 20036–4095
    Tel. (202)785.6323
Telex: 440245 WASHINGTON D.C.
Telefax: (202)785.0350

Venezuela
Libreria del Este
Avda F. Miranda 52, Aptdo. 60337
Edificio Galipan
Caracas 106
    Tel. 951.1705/951.2307/951.1297
Telegram: Libreste Caracas

Yugoslavia – Yougoslavie
Jugoslovenska Knjiga
Knez Mihajlova 2, P.O. Box 36
Beograd   Tel. 621.992
Telex: 12466 jk bgd

Orders and inquiries from countries where
Distributors have not yet been appointed
should be sent to: OECD Publications
Service, 2 rue André-Pascal, 75775 Paris
Cedex 16.
Les commandes provenant de pays où
l'OCDE n'a pas encore désigné de distributeur devraient être adressées à : OCDE,
Service des Publications, 2, rue André-Pascal, 75775 Paris Cedex 16.

1/90

OECD PUBLICATIONS, 2 rue André-Pascal, 75775 PARIS CEDEX 16
PRINTED IN FRANCE
(43 90 02 1) ISBN 92-64-13359-3 - No. 45145 1990